Shannon Jung

We Are Home

A Spirituality of the Environment

PAULIST PRESS
New York/Mahwah

Cover photograph by Jim Eckles.

Library of Congress Cataloging-in-Publication Data

Jung, Shannon, 1943–
    We are home: a spirituality of the environment/Shannon Jung.
      p. cm.
    Includes index.
    ISBN 0-8091-3364-4
    1. Human ecology—Religious aspects—Christianity.
  2. Spirituality. I. Title.
    BT695.5.J86   1993
    261.8′362—dc20   92-37876
                                                  CIP

Published by Paulist Press
997 Macarthur Boulevard
Mahwah, New Jersey 07430

Printed and bound in the
United States of America

Table of Contents

*To Patti—
home indeed.*

Preface

We camped in Colorado next to the Rocky Mountain National Park a couple of years ago. One thing that fascinated me there was the Rocky Mountain sheep. A medium-sized animal with great curving horns, these sheep are truly magnificent. Once native to the area they have almost become extinct. Now park personnel are going to great lengths to help them make a comeback. The Park Service even has signs on the road warning motorists that this is where the sheep cross from the mountain to their grazing meadow.

We found ways to be nearby when the sheep were reported to cross. The third day we got lucky. Around 9:00 a.m. we saw movement way up on the mountain. Ever so slowly the herd grazed its way down the steep slope. They are shy, bashful animals. Finally they worked themselves down to within 200 yards of the road.

All of a sudden a Greyline Tours bus roared up. It disgorged its passengers, loud and armed with cameras. The sheep froze. The people scared them; they had no history with the animals—not even my hour's worth.

The bus roared off even as it had arrived. In a few minutes the sheep continued down the mountain and crossed the road into their meadow. I felt privileged to have been there.

I was observant enough that day to appreciate my relatedness to the sheep. I had to a degree become part of their environment and they of mine. The tourists had encountered them only as scenery, external to themselves. However disruptive their behavior, the tourists were part of the environment. They had an influence.

This story illustrates my title. That day I realized I was not separate from the sheep, the mountains, the meadow. Rather I was part of the environment. My point is that humankind is not simply **at** home in the natural world; we **are** part of that home. Our bodily processes continuously interact with the atmosphere, with earth, with plants, with animals. We are natural.

What might our naturalness mean for a theology and ethics of the environment? I am persuaded that it has far-reaching implications that can substantially revise the way we think and act. It promises greater enjoyment of our lives in addition to a healthier environment for all living things.

A number of themes make this book somewhat distinctive. The foremost is that it takes our embodiment in space and time as an inescapable fact. We are enabled and uplifted by our physical nature. If we take this seriously we see that we are fellow travellers with the rest of nature. What might that mean for ethics and for theology?

A second related theme is that of God's presence in the world. There is a hidden ecological tradition whose representatives are being rediscovered. Who has heard, for example, of Hildevert of Lavardin, Archbishop of Tours in the eleventh century? He wrote: "God is over all things, under all things, outside all things, within, but not enclosed, without, but not excluded . . . wholly without, embracing, wholly within, filling."[1] Many familiar theologians have made related claims, but even their nuances of God's presence are only now being retrieved. What does it mean to claim the incarnation, to assert that the holy does dwell in the commonplace?

A less distinctive but consistent theme is that human flourishing has to be considered simultaneously with natural flourishing. Citing the Second Vatican Council and Pope

John Paul II, Archbishop John Roach emphasizes that "the proper ecological balance will not be found without directly addressing the structural forms of poverty that exist throughout the world."[2] The perspective offered here is that natural flourishing includes the well-being of the human species. Empathy with all others is the virtue appropriate to the interdependent world we live in.

Related to this is the debate about appropriate development. It is obvious that theories pitting Soviet socialism against U.S. capitalism have run their course. At least one school of thought is emerging that maintains that ecological sustainability is a vital aspect of development. To be successful, it claims, development strategies need to incorporate a concern for nature, for economic equity, and for participation, as well as for effectiveness in raising material living standards.[3]

Perhaps a brief comment is in order explaining why these pages are not crammed with statistics or overburdened with "should's." That is the result of my concern that this book be of assistance in helping us see the world as our home. Caring for the earth and its future will emerge out of a sense of nature as a sacrament; that sense will frame our response to statistics.[4] Similarly, ethics might be more sensitive to the psychological impact of moral language. Analytical critique and lists of obligations are all well and good, but they seldom motivate anyone to action. It is images and experiences that engage our imagination and move us.[5] It was, I believe, the Rocky Mountain sheep that got this book on track!

Finally, this book represents a gamble. It gambles that ethics will be more productive if human beings' relationships to each other are framed within an ecological context rather than the reverse—environmental ethics seen as secondary to human social ethics. The framework proposed here comprehends social inter-human ethics as an aspect of the web of environmental ethics. It invites the reader to see him or herself within that web of life.

My world is blessed with generous and constructive teachers. Let me acknowledge at least those most directly connected with this project. Students in courses in environmental ethics at Concordia College, Moorhead, Minnesota; Wartburg Seminary, and the University of Dubuque Seminary have questioned, argued, supported, and stimulated my thinking. Paul Peterson and Barbara Bullock-Tiffany have been particularly provocative.

The beauty I have enjoyed while hiking, camping, skiing, bicycling, and jogging—and also just sitting—has made the environment an enriching teacher. I rejoice that Michael, Robert, and Nathan enjoy that same beauty and kinship with the world, and want all other children to be able to do so as well.

My colleagues, Drs. Ralph Smith and Winston Persaud have all read the entire manuscript and offered insightful suggestions. Farmers, rural folks, and pastors have critiqued lectures out of which this material emerged during the course of my duties as Director of the Center for Theology and Land. A host of influential teachers may not even be aware that their thinking has found its way into these pages.

Teresa Peterson has, as usual, gone far beyond the minimum in processing the manuscript for this book.

Dick Sparks at Paulist Press has maintained contact with me and encouraged the writing while it was in process. That is editing at its relational best.

This book is dedicated to Dr. Patricia Beattie Jung, my colleague, wife, co-parent, and lover. I do know the meaning of providence.

1

Where We Are: Our Home

Each of us is an environment.
Our local environment is our body.
It is a body connected with other bodies—animal, human,
    celestial.
Even though we experience our environment/our body as
    local, it isn't.
We have a connection to every other environment; the
    environment moves through us; we modify the
    environment.
All of us are part of the environment.

Nothing has brought these ideas home to me more dramati-
cally than my own breathing. Every breath that you and I take
includes a billion molecules of oxygen that have come from
plants. These same molecules have been in the lungs of every
one of the 50 billion human beings who have ever lived.[1] The
essential act of breathing connects us with all of humanity. It
also connects us with plants and animals. It is an unconscious,
yet ever-so-familiar bond with people of every race, religion,
and culture. Breathing also connects us in a dynamic of dependency with plants, animals, and inorganic substances. All
of these influence and are influenced by carbon dioxide, oxygen—the atmosphere.
    Breathing figures prominently in the Hebrew scriptures'
story of how the world came into being. The second creation
story of Genesis (2:7) recounts that God formed "man of dust

from the ground, and **breathed** into his nostrils the **breath** of life; and man became a living being." Later, when the animals are going into the ark with Noah, the writer describes them as "two and two of all flesh in which there was the **breath** of life" (Gen 7:15; cf. 6:17). Psalm 104 includes all life in the metaphor of breath. "When you take away their **breath**, they fail and they return to the dust from which they came; but when you **breathe** into them, they recover" (Ps 104:29–30). The connection between human life and all creation is crystal clear to the author of Ecclesiastes. "They all draw the same **breath**. Humans have no advantage over beast" (Eccl 3:19). An interesting sidelight is that the word used in these passages also can be translated "spirit." The implication is that God breathes the spirit of life, God's own Spirit, into animals and into humankind.

Considering the scientific evidence about the omnipresence of molecules, it may be said that all living things breathe the breath of God! The same primordial molecules have animated organic life since the beginning of creation. But the larger recognition is that God is present in both the organic and the inorganic world, of which life is a part. This link is the emphasis of the Christian belief in creation. It is a belief exemplified by the incarnation of Jesus Christ.

These are the basic tenets of environmental ethics. They may not be the traditional beginning points for most Christians or other believers, but there is today a new openness towards a holistic theology and ethics which is reflected in these beliefs. I want to explore with you the destinations of these beliefs.

Fellow Travellers: Phytoplankton and Human

Let's begin with our home planet. Earth is a conglomerate of everyday miracles. Our bodies, and the other bodies that make up the earth, are fellow travellers on this sphere as it whirls though the universe. The interaction between these travellers is a story that captures our imagination.

The survival of the human species depends on the continued operation of a vast number of other systems and other species. These systems create a hyper-system, or biosphere. While our human breathing is inseparably linked to all the biosphere, at this point we narrow our focus to the link with a single species.

A humble benefactor of humans is the minuscule, single-celled plant species, phytoplankton. The giant of this species measures only a few thousandths of an inch across. Phytoplankton live on top of the ocean. Their environment goes only as far down as sunlight will penetrate. Phytoplankton drift with the currents and the tides. All sea-life is dependent on them. Through photosynthesis, phytoplankton convert carbon dioxide and water into carbohydrates, fats, and proteins—the food of life![2]

New types of microscopes have enabled scientists to discover whole classes of phytoplankton that were previously undetected. Sallie Chisholm, a biological oceanographer at MIT, says that the tiny plants were long mistaken for dirt. "We didn't think plants could be so small." Or so abundant. Chisholm and her colleagues recently discovered a species that populates the ocean in concentrations as high as three million per ounce.[3]

The diversity and number of these tiny plants are an indication of ecological strength. Their impact on the earth matches or exceeds that of rain forests. Carpets of these "plankters" span the world's oceans. Each year these trillions of plants draw out of the atmosphere almost half of the carbon dioxide put in by human and other animal species (3 of the 6 billion tons). In effect, the plankters prevent half of the annual output of carbon dioxide from reaching the upper atmosphere and contributing to global warming.

What isn't clear is how the plankters will react to increasing doses of carbon dioxide. Like plants in commercial greenhouses, the increased carbon dioxide might encourage their work. Conversely, a significant warming of the oceans might suppress their work. We don't know. Some scientists claim that the phytoplankton are appearing in fewer numbers than was estimated for southern oceans.

Another positive influence phytoplankton might have on the climate has nothing to do with carbon dioxide. Some plankters emit dimethyl sulfate as a defense against being poisoned by sea water. In the atmosphere this dimethyl sulfate converts to sulfate. Robert Charlson and James Lovelock suggest that those sulfate particles serve as the nuclei around which cloud droplets condense.[4] By multiplying the number of sunlight-scattering droplets, the particles increase the albedo (amount of light reflected back to space) of the earth. This contributes to a cooling effect. Overall, phytoplankton—to the extent that we presently understand their operation—act in ways that sustain animal and human life.

The plankters' impact on the sustainability of climate and food supply is remarkable. They also have incredible abilities within their single cell to adapt to environmental fluctuations. At present we do not know whether their capabilities can keep pace with the demands that human pollution places on them. Actually, the adaptive capacities of the phytoplankton may have more impact on the Earth's future than do our own, human actions!

Breathing

This humble species, through its activity, enables humankind to continue breathing. We seldom think about breathing except when it becomes problematic, for instance when we are in high altitudes. But the necessity of breathing is such that without air we would suffer irreversible brain damage in five minutes. In contrast, we can live for a week without water, and a month without food. Breathing is elemental.

From our first cry at birth to our final exhalation, nothing is more important or more routine than our breathing. Twelve to sixteen times a minute (while at rest) our diaphragm rises and falls, the muscles of the rib cage expand and contract, and we breathe. Normally **each** breath brings a half liter of air into our lungs; during strenuous exercise that amount can rise to 6.5 liters. We inhale from six to 104 liters of air each minute.[5]

From this perspective the quality of that air matters a great deal. We are creatures who by necessity draw elements of the environment into ourselves. So the quality of that environment is vital.

Nevertheless, it is wrong to assume that our bodies are helpless victims of whatever they draw in from the environment. Indeed, the human body is miraculous in its ability to filter out toxic and noxious elements. Three organ systems serve as filters or screens between body and biosphere—the respiratory tract, the gastrointestinal tract, and the skin. Since we have already discussed breathing, the respiratory tract will remain our focus.

After inhaling, air is the subject of an extensive cleansing process. First, it is screened crudely by nostril hairs for larger matter particles. Contact with moist spaces in the nose warms and humidifies the air which facilitates the release of oxygen into the blood stream. Soluble gases begin dissolving as soon as they enter the moist respiratory tract. Since air usually doesn't need to penetrate deeply into the lungs, waste tends to be deposited on nasal passages and the throat. The nose and throat are lined with special cells that trap other particulate matter with a sticky mucus. This is what we expel when we blow our nose.

Throughout the respiratory tract are other filtering agents—tiny hairlike growths called cilia. Their vibrations trap toxic agents and push them back up to be coughed out or ingested. From the larynx (just below the throat) and on down, the respiratory tract resembles an upside-down tree. As the passageways go down, they become smaller and smaller, more and more refining. They end in alveoli, a passageway resembling a cluster of grapes. The business of transferring oxygen into the blood and waste carbon dioxide out of the blood takes place here.

By carrying oxygen-rich hemoglobin to other organs the bloodstream allows the oxidation reactions that release the energy needed to fuel growth, motion, and other bodily functions. The heat, water, carbon dioxide, and other wastes created by those reactions are eventually eliminated. The air we exhale, for example, contains six percent less oxygen and five or six percent more carbon dioxide than it did when we inhaled it.

The respiratory system, like phytoplankton, is remarkably well-equipped to interact with its environment. Our respiratory organs screen, filter, and make use of the air that sustains us. Like animal and plant systems, the respiratory system takes in the usable and life-sustaining elements of our environment and then excretes wastes and toxins.

Air Quality

Since the Industrial Revolution, these extraordinary respiratory systems have had to deal with the modern phenomenon of air pollution. Air pollution not only causes billions of dollars in property damage and lost crops, but also death and disease. For as long as we continue to burn significant amounts of fossil fuels—a demand created by our technology and life-style choices—the need to control pollutants will remain with us.

A serious threat is posed by the possible impact of a simple everyday gas called carbon dioxide. Carbon dioxide occurs naturally in the atmosphere. It forms a fraction of every breath we and other animals take. Conversely, all life in the plant kingdom takes in carbon dioxide and emits oxygen. This is part of the admirable synergy which allows life to continue on the planet.

Breathing is not the only source of carbon dioxide in the biosphere, however. Combustion of all types of fossil fuel also releases CO_2. Any kind of combustion—e.g., campfires or burning leaves—gives off carbon dioxide. It is the enormous amount of combustion occurring in industrialized societies which is creating the real problem. Carbon dioxide is increasing at a far more rapid pace than can be absorbed by plants—including the humble phytoplankton.

Carbon dioxide levels in the atmosphere have been steadily rising during this century. In the atmosphere carbon dioxide—and other gases—allow high-frequency solar radiation to pass through the atmosphere to the surface of earth, but then they trap the lower-frequency, reflected heat. These functions of the atmosphere can be accurately compared to a giant greenhouse. The same greenhouse dynamic has, ironically, permitted life on earth to develop and thrive.

The release of CO_2 by the burning of carbon-based fuels such as oil, gas, and coal has been steadily increasing. This growth is especially evident in developing countries, even though the United States, the Commonwealth of Independent States, and China remain the largest contributors of carbon emissions. **In addition**, the denuding of tropical rain forests throughout the world has decreased the planet's ability to recycle carbon dioxide. Whatever the cause, global warming is real. The fact that the biosphere's homeostasis (natural balance) is being upset cannot be denied. Will a new and just as livable homeostasis emerge? We don't know.

The effect of carbon dioxide on the environment and thus on our health is hard to ignore. Some of the results of the global warming trend can even be projected. A current estimate is that the average temperature of the planet will increase by 5.5° F by 2030.[6] As the air warms it is able to hold more moisture, and therefore it is projected that precipitation will increase 7–11%. Increased temperature, however, also means increased evaporation. This could lead to drier soils in farm belts, which presents a bleak future for the world's food supply.

A major fear is the rise of sea levels, the result of melting polar ice. If temperatures were to rise the expected 5.5° F, it is estimated that sea levels would rise by 2½ feet. Since nearly a third of all humans live within 37 miles of a coastline, a rise in sea level will cause mass migrations from coastal regions.[7]

Intensifying the effects of higher levels of carbon dioxide are greater concentrations of other so-called "greenhouse gases"—notably methane, chlorofluorocarbons (CFC's), and nitrous oxide. These gases are both more potent and increasing more rapidly. They have as much potential as CO_2 to warm the atmosphere.[8]

This non-CO_2 warming occurs as those chemicals deplete the ozone layer surrounding the planet. Used in aerosols, foam insulation, solvents, air conditioning, refrigeration, and flexible foam, CFC's are deeply embedded in our daily use. Besides the hole in the ozone layer over Antarctica that has been appearing since 1979, the ozone layer **around the entire globe** is eroding much faster than models had predicted.[9] Furthermore, the amount of this erosion reflects only the influence of gases released through the early 1980's. Because it takes years for these gases to reach the stratosphere, the situation will get much worse before any worldwide ban on CFC's can have an impact.

Since ozone blocks some harmful ultraviolet rays from reaching the earth's surface by absorbing them, one of the effects of ozone depletion is an increase in skin cancers. Researchers also fear that ultraviolet rays depress human immunological response.[10] Finally, ultraviolet radiation penetrates several meters in clear water and threatens many aquatic organisms, including our friend the phytoplankton.

A climate of human invention, the political climate, is also influenced by the change in the environment. The levels of pollution discovered in eastern Europe, and especially some towns in former East Germany where children had to be evacuated for their respiratory health for two months each summer, were shocking. At the same time the realization that carbon dioxide emissions are accelerating most rapidly in developing countries raises tough ethical questions. Do we (the developed world) ask eastern European and developing countries to adhere to stringent environmental standards that impede their short-term (at least) economic development? Can we justify freezing national standards of living around the globe at their present levels? Will there be economic restrictions on those nations that contribute most to the degeneration of the environment? As these questions indicate, just and effective solutions seem almost beyond reach, **yet they are simultaneously vital**.

Our recounting the story of the phytoplankton and their connection to our health and the quality of the atmosphere ends here. We have focused mainly on one creature's relationship to one other species—the human. We have seen how our bodily health is dependent on environmental quality, with a particular emphasis on one organ system—the respiratory tract. We have been introduced to carbon dioxide. However, the interconnection between all the aspects of the eco-chain makes it impossible to fully discuss even these narrow subjects. The bio-system in which humans are involved includes many other species and elements. We could have started with another species, could have emphasized other bodily systems, and could have dealt with other pollutants (e.g., water pollution, soil contamination, waste disposal).

All systems, environmental and life-style, are interconnected. Our dependence on fossil fuels, which generate CO_2, and on refrigeration and air conditioning, which use gases that deplete the ozone layer, are tied into our daily expectations. U.S. American, Canadian, western European and Japanese life-styles powerfully seduce the citizens of other countries.

Human Response

No advantage is gained by feeling personally guilty about global warming. You didn't produce global warming trends yourself. No one person has. However, personal responsibility is still an issue to be dealt with, even though it gets complicated.

For instance, a few weeks ago I noticed that the cooling system in my 1978 Toyota wagon was only "fanning the air." I took it in to a local service station, where an attendant added 3 quarts of freon to the air-conditioning system. When the manager of the station gave me the bill, he explained that there was $1.80 tax on each quart. "Next year," he said, "you won't be able to buy it at all. They're developing a new gas which will be much more expensive. EPA regulations."

My initial reaction, I blush to say, was to wonder whether my newer van also needed freon. Could I stockpile some by adding freon now? My impulse was not to stop depleting ozone but to avoid personal expense, avoid inconvenience, and maintain my personal comfort level. Only secondarily was I glad to hear that the federal government was working to combat the emission of CFC's, and was doing that in a way that would impact **all** U.S. citizens equally. I can accept personal expense or inconvenience for a good cause if I know that the impact is egalitarian in practice. We have to **start** with egalitarian approaches if we are to heighten perceptions of the significance of environmental concerns. Changed perceptions are where we begin to reverse the effects of environmental pollution.

A shift of perspective has begun. Major grocery stores are carrying products that are environmentally friendly. The response to the 20th anniversary of Earth Day and to the Earth Summit in Rio de Janeiro indicated that the environment has ceased to be a fringe issue. Certainly ecology is becoming a more central concern in Christian churches. Supporting and expanding this shift in perception is the major purpose of this book.

An incredible array of resources exist for the purpose of improving our environmental health. Human ingenuity is doubtless our biggest resource. If all humanity is persuaded that the struggle for environmental health is a matter of life and death, then humans can gradually learn how to live symbiotically with the biosphere. If we move quickly enough, most life support systems can still be sustained.

Gerald Barney offers two scenarios for the near future.[11] He sees the possibility of an earth that is much hotter, that experiences frequent floods and droughts, an earth in which sunlight itself is life-threatening. In this scenario four-fifths of the world lives in hopeless poverty. Once-fertile cropland has turned into arid wastelands, resulting in starvation and mass death. The industrialized one-fifth of the world attempts to maintain a state based on military power and uses that power to acquire resources (especially coal and uranium) from other nations. It is a future of an elite few living in great opulence supported by a vastly increased dependence on drugs.

But Barney sees another possible scenario. It is a scenario in which the protection of the planet's life support system has become a top priority in every nation. Brilliant minds and budget dollars have been converted away from military purposes to find ways of obtaining the greatest possible benefits from every resource used. Developing countries have been assisted with technical and educational aid. The entire world has learned to live within their social and environmental limits. Policies based on the long-term health of the planet are the norm, not the exception.[12]

If we accept Barney's scenarios, it seems clear that, at this moment, humanity is standing at the fork in the road. In 1983 Skjei and Whorton wrote that "we are forced over and over again to wonder if life on earth isn't in as much danger of being irrevocably poisoned by the substances [our] cultures manufacture . . . as it is of being vaporized in a thermonuclear war."[13]

From the perspective of the 1990's, it seems clear that we **do** have a **greater** chance of being irrevocably poisoned. Every day our life support systems are being destroyed by human activity, **but there are signs of hope**. The Christian faith has powerful resources to offer in the movement to step away from poisoning ourselves and all life. Christianity has a perspective which can be therapeutic in promoting the healing process. It is particularly important that churches join other partners on an equal footing. Though the church's reasons for environmental action are distinctive and significant, these reasons counsel us to recognize that it is the life of the **whole** world that is God's life.

Outline of the Book

Let me indicate where the argument of this book is going. If we are to be effective in communicating the impact of environmental issues on our future, we will need to understand what forces have produced the present, diseased state of the environment. Chapter 2 looks at the social-political, economic, life-style, psychological, and intellectual reasons for our present dilemmas. We will gain a better perspective on needed changes by attending to the dynamics that have brought us to the present impasse.

Chapter 3 suggests that the environmental situation is in fact a religious issue, that God is very much involved in the environment. It asserts that unless we can gain a transcendent vantage point on the importance of the planet for all life, our chances of reversing the fortunes of our biosphere are slim. My conviction is that there are heretofore untapped resources in the Christian faith that are especially persuasive in this effort.

Chapter 4 articulates a spiritual vision of the earth as God's home and ours. The fifth chapter considers the relationship between the human species and the rest of the created order in light of the theological vision formulated in chapter 4. In addressing the relationship among human beings as well as with other species, the fifth chapter suggests that equal regard for other persons is essential to environmental regeneration.

The sixth chapter builds on the arguments of the preceding two. It asks, "If this is God's home (chapter 4) and this is who we are at home (5), what sort of homemaking is appropriate?" It addresses the question of ethics.

Chapter 7 faces a relationship too often shunted to one side: the relation between organisms and their material needs—economics. We humans will need to address economic questions in an ecologically healthy way. That is vital.

Throughout these chapters the human relationship to God will be the foundation on which the other relations are based; in effect, the relation to God will ground and shape the others.

The epilogue will offer some ways in which we human beings can act to bring about the recovery of environmental health. It will focus particularly on the church's role in eco-praxis—a role that can be renewing for many aspects of the church's life and mission.

2

How Did We Get Here?

Your reaction to the story of our/God's/the phytoplankton's breathing may be:

It all gets too big; I can't deal with it.

Welcome to the club! We all feel that way sometimes. The good news is:

You don't have to feel that way.

I have a small card in my bathroom that I see every morning when I shave. It says:

"You are not absolutely, irrevocably, personally responsible for everything. That's my job."
Love, God.

A little corny, perhaps, but it helps those of us who are obsessive-compulsive. The theology's pretty good as well.

When we think about the state of the environment we get tired. There's just so much environment to think about and every day there are fresh revelations about the effect of some new chemical or the loss of some species. It's overwhelming—so overwhelming, in fact, that we become psychically numbed and immobilized. It reminds me of Jonathan Schell's claim in

The Fate of the Earth[1]—incidentally, not a bad title for a book on environmental ethics. His claim was that the enormity of the consequences of nuclear war is psychically numbing. It prevents us from thinking about how to avoid that possibility.

The same thing happens in regard to the diseased state of the environment. We simply shut down. We feel, and are encouraged to feel, responsible for restoring the entire planet to good health. And we know—when we think about it—that we can't do that. But we may shut down our reflective capacities long before we consciously realize that we can't rejuvenate all natural processes single-handedly. We just **feel** guilty—our guilt generators are revving at 6000 rpm and we are not getting anywhere, just feeling bad.

In addition to guilt, we sometimes get the sense that human beings are basically a greed-engorged, malevolent lot who wantonly ravage the beauty of nature with no thought for other species or even our own. Teilhard de Chardin said that the biggest tragedy that could befall us was that the human race would fall out of love with itself.[2] In some ways we have done exactly that. Some environmental advertising and the promotion campaigns of some environmental groups seem intended to make us feel bad about being human. We are pictured as environmental criminals.[3]

That doesn't make the problem go away. Instead, it shifts the problem from outside (pollution) to inside (guilt and self-loathing). To the extent that we buy into those cynical and despairing images we become further immobilized. The production of feelings of guilt and species-hatred are not going to clean up one particle of particulate matter or save one phytoplankton.

In this book I take the perspective that has helped me avoid immobilizing guilt in dealing with the degeneration of the environment.

No single individual is responsible for the state of the natural world.

Only God sustains, oversees, and renews the world.

God has chosen to work through individuals and communities to do this.

I **am** responsible for my contribution to the health of the environment individually and through my communities.

Further, God cares for the species **homo sapiens** at least as much as any other species. We are valuable to God, to each other, and to other species. It is out of a deep love and concern for our own kind and the whole of our home planet that we can respond to what happens to our biosphere. We are fellow travellers. What happens to one, happens to all.

If we can avoid paralyzing (and responsibility-displacing!) guilt individually and corporately, then we can get on with dealing with the ecofuture. It will be a useful perspective to understand that, though the process has quickened, environmental deterioration has been going on a long time. We are simply the first generation to discover that we have the capacity to destroy our life-support system.[4] We also have a fair amount of confidence that we can reverse the decline of that system.

This makes the topic of our present chapter all the more significant—how did we get here? What accounts for the present state of our world? How did humankind manage to relate to nature in such a way as to produce the dreadful situation all living things now find themselves in? And, perhaps the most important question, **what prevents us from being more environmentally responsible**? Answering these questions—or having a crack at them—will assuage our guilt by showing how deeply institutionalized and historical are the causes of the present situation.[5] It will also begin to suggest those areas that require transformation in moving toward a healthy future.

We will begin by looking at the present attitudes and experiences which prevent us from being better eco-citizens. We will then try to locate the roots of those attitudes and habits. In effect, we will be moving from a catalog of present impediments or symptoms—the visible plant—to the long-term causes of our dilemma—the deep roots. In this way we may begin to see that problematic attitudes and structures arise out of the same soil, and need to be addressed together.

Lack of Knowledge and Power

"I just don't know enough about how to make a difference. The problems seem so overwhelming and I don't have clear alternatives to choose from."

At first my assessment was that there couldn't be anyone in the United States or any other literate country that didn't know about environmental dangers. Every magazine, newspaper, news broadcast, bookstore, and television show is full of information.

When I appeal to lack of knowledge, what that frequently means is that I don't choose to learn more. That just puts off the question we are dealing with here; that is, transforms it into a question about why I or others don't care enough to learn more. However, on closer examination this seems to open out onto two other, related and serious issues: it expresses a pervasive sense of individualism and also of powerlessness. "How could I hope to make a difference?" There is even in the question a discounting of oneself, as well as an implied belief that only **individuals** can make a difference. The thing that surprised me most on a 1989 trip to Zimbabwe and South Africa, two countries stymied by poverty and racial oppression, was their sense of hope for the future. That hope —in the face of considerable odds—derived from a sense of communal solidarity with others. I came back hungry to find out what those words—communal solidarity—really signify.

Any solutions to environmental problems will require addressing the issues of powerlessness and individualism. The roots of those social dynamics are too deep, too complex to do more than note their sources here. The book by Robert Bellah and company, *Habits of the Heart*, gave us an update on the robust health of individualism in this country. The attention that the book received indicated that it had accurately described a feature of contemporary America. The concepts of individualism and powerlessness have been associated with modernity so much that we almost assume that the two go together.[6] That may be particularly true in a country which bases its system of politics and economics on a tradition of individual rights and responsibilities. This is often reflected as well in a western Christian view of individual salvation and an emphasis on personally choosing to have a relationship with Jesus. All in all, there are structural and attitudinal forces that keep individualism alive and well.

The pendulum may be swinging back toward a greater appreciation of community. While those who write the books and do the broadcasts, the "opinion-makers," are part of the baby boomer generation that most emphasized individualism, personal autonomy, and self-expressive values, a huge segment of the United States population continues to emphasize local neighborhood, family, and community.[7] There are also those culture analysts, like Gibson Winter, who discern a deepening communal sensibility and interdependence. We may be realizing that we **are** part of an ecological community, that we cannot choose to be otherwise. This transformation is evident in ecological and religious movements that are challenging individualistic patterns.[8] Some theological writers are confronting the sense of powerlessness. Not only are they members of feminist, ecological, or liberation movements; some are addressing middle class powerlessness.[9]

Everything I have said should suggest that this first reason, lack of knowledge and power, is a very real detriment to environmental health. We need information; we need real alternatives to products that are pollutants, and to life-styles that are destructive. **But what we need most is a sense that we can make a difference together.**

Any hoped-for reversal in the decline of this environment in which we live and breathe is dependent upon a realistic alternative to a sense of individual powerlessness. My guess is that this disease is ultimately a spiritual malady which calls for a religious alternative. That just may be emerging.

Our Economic System and Consumer Costs

"It would be wonderful if I could be environmentally more sensitive. However, it's just too complicated and expensive to do all the things that are eco-friendly. I just don't have the time to recycle my garbage, or ride a bicycle to work, much less do without air conditioning or refrigeration. I can barely imagine that. In terms of both time and money, it's too expensive."

This may be the most popular impediment in the sense that ecological responsibility seems too expensive to us. We think of ecology and economics as contradictory rather than complementary spheres. Frankly, as modern economics are presently arranged, they usually are.

At root, we fear that our life-styles will be severely threatened if we begin to adopt more environmentally-healthy practices. For example, in going grocery shopping, we could resolve to use as little nonbiodegradable plastic as possible by taking paper bags to the supermarket and reusing them. We could ask for paper rather than plastic bags at the check-out line, or we could reuse our own cardboard boxes. But then how do we get rid of the garbage at the end of the week? Buy plastic garbage bags? Just throw everything, even the wet garbage, into paper bags? Well, we could use large garbage cans, recycle and compost wet garbage, separate out . . . and so forth. It all gets very complicated and time-consuming, and requires a lot of thought and care. The point is that our economy is not arranged for that.

In all honesty, we are taught that taking time and caring is not a very efficient use of our energy and, in the case of waste disposal, not worth our effort. It is not "billable time." Our life-styles are organized for efficiency, comfort, and convenience. For example, total farm income in 1985 was $28 billion; the total expense of packaging food that year was $29 billion.[10] The disparity is even greater today. Unfortunately, the values which such a life-style promotes often exclude not only the health of the planet, but our own health, as well. Why do we hunger and thirst after fast foods which damage both our bodily health and the environment's as well?[11] What all becomes part of our digestive tract and hemoglobin in the name of convenience? How does our own health get factored out simultaneously with the health of the natural world?

These life-style choices are **not** random or freely chosen nor do they grow out of a holistic view of human fulfillment. They are shaped by our western economy and its supporting institutional arrangements—most notably, the media and a pervasive religion of success/achievement/affluence. **The primary values of the economy are production and consumption.**

These values sustain economic growth which is the mechanism on which our system is based, and by which criteria any corporation or the economy as a whole is judged.

Clearly, we consumers are encouraged to buy the products of the system. Since we have certain limits on the amount of food we can eat and the number of cars we can drive, the media and socially institutionalized attitudes encourage us to upscale our dietary habits and automobiles. It is assumed that we will continue to consume in more sophisticated and expensive ways. The engines of the economy are designed to push production and consumption. Frugality and saving are discouraged.

What is obscured here is that, in defining ourselves as consumers, we essentially lose a sensitivity to the physical aspects of ourselves, which are intimately interrelated with other aspects of nature. Our dependence on breathing, surveyed in chapter 1, is a prime example. Too high a setting on the degree to which we identify with what we consume causes us to lose touch with our bodily well-being. We begin to think that our physical and mental health is something that we buy —a "consumable"—rather than something that we essentially are and do. Little wonder that we lose touch with the external environment when we have become cut off from our physical selves. We will come back to consideration of this relationship, but must also note a corollary result of it: we tend to lose touch with others and the extent to which our identity is interdependent with theirs.[12]

Our economy clearly influences and is influenced by the environment. Nevertheless, the economy fails to factor into the cost of production the changes that the processes of production make in the environment. The costs of air pollution, thermal water pollution, waste disposal, and energy source depletion are beginning to be felt, but they are externalized from the costs of goods.[13] The failure to cost out ecological results reinforces the individualism which is at the base of an emphasis on consumption and also of efficiency.[14] Although it's much harder to factor air/water/land costs **per capita** than to factor the costs to the bioregion corporately, nevertheless it is **local** governments   ʳᵃl consumers who **do** pay for landfills into which are   ner diapers, recyclable and non-recyclable plastics   items which produce profits for specific con anies.   economic incentive yet for corporatio   to do rese   eco-friendly products. I am persua d that day is no.

The fact that env   onmental costs and   so seldom enter pricing   dicates how little we app "placenta of life." It si   als, at the least, a lack of sensi. the ways in which ou   ives are bound together as a spec. with other life-forms   Ve treat the environment as a commons which can be co   inuously used without negative result. We assume that there   ll always be more air, water, and land. However, the limits   our future are coming into focus. I assess that as a sign o real hope.

Many social dynamics have caused us to view ecological health as an economic disaster. How did we come to regard the health of the environment as a luxury, as a disposable item? Are the health of the environment and the health of the economy **necessarily** opposed? These questions go to the core of the ecological question.

It is particularly distressing that Christian theology and ethics has offered little in the way of a serious alternate economic vision. There are very powerful social and intellectual reasons for this, not the least of which is that too frequently the church has accommodated the economic system. My opinion is that our economy and life-styles have been formed in a way that systematically ignores environmental impact.

Furthermore, the Christian faith has offered little of substance to an interpretation, much less guidance, of economics since the Enlightenment. The Christian faith has largely accommodated (or ignored) prevailing economic and ecological values. It has thereby abdicated some of its responsibility in addressing this second deep-seated reason for nonchalance about the environment. Any reversal of environmental deterioration will have to incorporate an alternate economic base, such as the one initiated in the Bishops' Pastoral on the Economy. It is especially important that the Christian faith integrate an economic dimension into its theology of the environment, as this book does in chapter 7.

Humankind Seen as Not Part of Environment

"The environment's just not that important; it doesn't affect me that much. Sure, the weather matters, but the environment's not central to who I am or to who other human beings are. What matters is how well I think and work, and my relationships with other people."

Stated as boldly as that, this reason may seem artificial or unrealistic. I am persuaded, however, that while not a conscious and certainly not a defensible reason, the sense that the environment really doesn't matter is very deeply embedded in our western, industrialized culture. Furthermore, the roots of this attitude are so deep that the attitude itself has become part of our language. For example, consider the way that we speak and write about everything in nature that is not human; even to make the point that human beings are part of nature, we refer to "human nature" which renders everything else "nonhuman nature." That seems to separate human beings from nature, and certainly from other species, even in the effort not to. For this reason some have advocated using "creation" instead of "nature"; the latter term is more easily objectified and impersonalized. We are trapped in language.

It is becoming abundantly evident, however, that what affects the natural world *does* affect humankind as part of that natural world. How then did we come to deny that? Modern science and technology have had some influence in reinforcing this denial, as we shall see in the next section. At present, however, we can identify the problem as arising on a number of fronts: seeing ourselves as separated into minds and bodies, i.e., body-mind dualism; the presence of humanocentric attitudes; and secularization.

Basically all these forces have contributed to the disconnection of men and women from nature. They have weakened what is an integral constitution of men and women as natural species to the status of an occasional relation.

For some time, especially in western countries, a division has existed which runs through the way people look at themselves. They think of themselves as bodies and minds which are joined together in some way, but which seldom genuinely interpenetrate. Human beings are identified with their minds, their thinking capacity, and their spirits—all terms popularly used interchangeably. That is who human beings **really** are. They simply find themselves in this medium called a body. The body, physical constitution, and nature—again interchangeable terms—are not really central to the self. This may explain why physical education is seen as peripheral in public schools.

In other interpretations, some of them Christian, the body is identified as "the flesh" and is seen as evil. Out of bodily depths erupt desires which are to be controlled and sublimated. Rarely in modern thought is the body or the material world seen as equally good as the mind or spirit. The material world, including the natural, physical aspects of ourselves, is depreciated and along with it the environment. The material world, including our bodies, came to be seen as raw material under the control of our minds and spirits. We think of ourselves as essentially just not natural. Rather, we think, we are **above** nature.[15]

The view that human beings transcend the rest of the world has been used to justify our using the material world in whatever ways we chose. Both our cultural and theological assumptions have placed humanity at the center of purpose and meaning in the universe. As Wesley Granberg-Michaelson writes, "A decisive evolution in modern thought has concluded that humanity's autonomous goals and purposes are the chief end of creation."[16] The value of any species is seen as its value to humanity; the cost of any venture is its human cost. Theologically we have made a similar assumption. Since the Renaissance we have assumed that God's relationship **to humankind** was the lens through which we should view all questions of value. Humanity's use of the environment for its own purposes, even if that included exploitation and destruction, could thereby be rationalized on theological grounds. The real counterbalance to exploitation has been the necessity of preserving the material world for the use of the human species in the future.

Fortunately some theologians have been questioning the assumptions of this humanocentrism. I think particularly of James Gustafson who asserts that we should relate to the material world as God relates to it, suggesting that the purpose of the world is not limited to human use:

> The purposes of the divine governance are, insofar as human beings can discern them, not exhausted by its benefits for us . . . they are not all directed toward us.[17]

There are voices which suggest that humankind is not the sole arbiter of value in the universe, and that the species is part of the entire web of creation. Eastern Orthodox perspectives, for example, clearly locate humanity within the natural world.

The fragmentation of the human is also coming to be seen as a misconception. Our thinking processes could not exist without bodily ones. They are interconnected. We are one. The depreciation of the material world and its separation from substantial connection with the self was accompanied by a suppression of women. Being seen as more closely connected with nature than men are, women have suffered from that association and from the culture's appreciation of the spiritual and mental to the detriment of the physical and material. The nature-spirit dichotomy simply does not make much sense to those who give birth and know both the joy and the pain of physicality. The suppression of women's perspectives furthered the separation of body from mind, nature from spirit.[18] That supported the fiction that human beings were not constitutionally part of the world of nature.

No longer.

Unqualified Faith in Science and Technology

"I know that there are environmental problems, but before they get too bad, our scientists will find a technical way to take care of them. Look at the things that we can do these days, thanks to science and technology. Besides, there will always be enough land, air, and water to take care of our needs."

If one looks at the track record of science and technology it is easy to see how a person might develop this sentiment. Indeed, we have benefitted enormously from scientific discoveries and the technological application of those discoveries.

My father has a pacemaker. My children were vaccinated against a multitude of diseases. My wife and I love our computer. Our home gives evidence of any number of gadgets that make our lives more pleasant and healthful. Science and technology are not the cause of our environment's loss of purity. However, an unbridled faith in science and technology's ability to extend the carrying capacity of the planet is just flat idolatrous.

As we stated earlier, science has helped promote a dualism between nature and spirit. Ivor Leclerc argues that a fundamental dualism has existed from the seventeenth century to the present in which physical existence was conceived as material, and excluded "perception, thought, feeling, emotion, etc."[19] In effect, the material world was identified as the province of the natural scientist; in the division of tasks philosophy and theology were assigned the mental and spiritual realms.[20] Theology capitulated its role in understanding and interpreting the material world of science, nature, and body.

These and other scientific assumptions of the past have caused great damage to the environment. The scientific description of the world in mechanical terms, the image of science as a detached and objective search for truth, and the atomistic bias of the sciences are factors which led to the depreciation of the material world.

Together these scientific proclivities tended to reinforce a technology which saw nature as something separate from humankind to be used however we pleased. The costs of that attitude to the environment are all around us. The emergence of the science of ecology testifies to the decline of an unqualified faith in science and technology. More and more science understands that the environment is a living part of ourselves. We cannot hope to control nature. We hope to live in harmony with our home.

A good example of this is the area of sustainable agriculture, a technology in which farmers use organic fertilizers and pesticides and crop rotation in a way that serves to sustain the health of the soil. It involves as few petrochemical inputs as possible, inputs which are contaminating the ground water we humans drink, the streams we fish in, and the fish. This is a real technology based on real scientific discoveries but it is driven by values other than growth and efficiency as conventionally understood. It also recognizes that there are natural sources of wisdom whose dynamics we need to understand. Finally, sustainable agriculture is based on a qualification of science and technology—there are limits to its capacities— and also on the recognition that the health of the environment is our health.

Environment Not a Central Concern of Christianity

"Sure, God loves us. That is the central message of Christianity; look at all God provided for us. God's real concern is with human beings; the environment is what God gave us. We have been taught that we should take care of the world, but the health of the environment is not really central. After all, the work of Jesus Christ and the Holy Spirit is totally directed toward men and women, not toward the world of nature."

Some critics would say that my characterization of this cause of our eco-neglect is far too charitable to Christianity. They would say that in fact Christianity has not just ignored the environment. It has encouraged technological development, economic growth, and a this-worldliness which has redounded to the ill-health of the biosphere.[21] Maybe they are right. My perspective is that Christianity has depended on a far too shallow theology and ethics of stewardship to express its theology of creation. There has been such a pale alternative to the prevailing theology of human benevolence that the environment slipped to the margins of Christian concern. Happily there is some evidence of a turnabout.

The charge is that Christianity has aggravated the other four trends we have described, usually unwittingly. Christian theology has simply not had a very central concern for the environment. **The primary culprit, in my opinion, is the separation that Christianity fostered between God and nature, as well as between humanity and nature**. Stephen Toulmin has located some of the roots of this separation:

> The seventeenth-century transition—from the animated, active cosmos of the medieval natural philosophers to the inert, **de**animated, material world of the new mathematical philosophy—was only one of a series of dichotomies, which ended not just by dividing mind from matter, [divinity from bodily creatures], rational thought from causal process, but by separating the realm of "values" from that of "facts" and setting **Humanity** over against **Nature**.[22]

Toulmin indicates that an even greater division between God and nature took place by showing how, **only** with the scientific revolution, did the divine realm become the World of **Supernature** rather than that of nature. Only then did "Acts of God" involve a suspension of natural laws and intervention "**from outside**."[23] Our theology of nature is seriously underdeveloped as a result of its long history of segregation and depreciation.

The upshot of this was to separate God from creation. What resulted was a deist-watchmaker view of God in relation to the environment. While Christians affirmed that God was intimately involved with humankind, they too often understood the future of the rest of creation as being left to human stewardship. Because God has not been seen as intimately involved with nature, human stewardship has come to have an only-secondary moral or theological significance.

One implication of this view which carries considerable wallop is that God no longer cares for creation. God simply made the world and left it to its own natural laws and humanity's care. What is being expressed here is not only the humanocentrism we encountered earlier but also the view that nature is basically inert, an object to be used. That is very far from the biblical view. It **does** help us understand how the environment came to be seen as not one of God's or Christianity's major concerns.

The predominance of neo-orthodox theology continued this trend. With its emphasis on the personal relation between God and human beings rather than on the structures of existence, neo-orthodoxy unconsciously downplayed societal determination and physical reality. It often fed into the view of human beings as transcending the environment. God dwelt and related to human beings in the personal realm of the spirit.[24]

This view spurned a realistic view of natural limitation. It tended to trivialize the need to transform structures. Interestingly, it played into the culture's appreciation of technological progress or at least acquiesced in that development. The environment was, after all, not where the "real" human being lived.

Moreover, it assumed that since God operated only through personal relations, the structures of the material and structural world could have little to teach us. God's revelation simply did not operate on that frequency. The seeds planted by an uncritical acceptance of western culture and technology have resulted in environmental destruction, technological breakdowns, and great suffering in the Two-Thirds world. We are witnessing the results of not listening to creation. The environment has a voice that requires sensitivity on the part of the hearer, but too often theology has excluded that voice. The consequences of a theological and cultural expulsion of nature from history still hover over us.

Another factor which has permitted this to continue is the christocentric character of much contemporary theology. The model of the divine relationship with humanity is to be found in the life of Jesus Christ. "The new reality, constituting men and women as such, was the active relation of the one with the other, reflecting and responding to God's relation to us in the other who is Jesus Christ."[25] The stress fell on interpersonal relations, a stress which has of course dominated Christian ethics. This central emphasis, legitimate in itself, effectively excluded the relationship of dependency that **does in fact** exist between human beings and their environment. What appears to be needed is a wider interpretation that includes the physical and non-personal realms. As theological matters now stand, the widespread discomfort with the nature-spirit dichotomy may or may not seem vital enough to generate more eco-friendly theological thinking. We can encourage such thinking.

Conclusion

While I am sure there are other sources explaining our relative neglect of the environment, most of those are related to the five impediments we have examined here. It may be helpful to consider what links these five areas:

- individualism and powerlessness;
- the economic system and our life-styles;
- a view that human beings are not really part of nature;
- an almost-unqualified faith in science and technology to fix things; and

■ a view that the environment is not central to God or to Christians.

None of the five has simply opposed the health of the environment. In no case has there been a suggestion that the ecosphere is not at all important, just that its importance has been secondary to other concerns. What has happened, however, is that a different model of human life and activity has been in ascendancy since the time of the Enlightenment. **The predominant and most influential feature of that model is its confidence in the premier position of the human subject in the cosmos.**

If that is the case, and perhaps it is almost axiomatic to say so, then what does that imply for our concern? It would seem to suggest that the model of the human which has downplayed the environment is a model that is basically unnatural. Unnatural in a particular way, however.

The ascendant model has been that of the unconnected human.

Not unconnected to God. Not unconnected to a disembodied mind or spirit.

But certainly not connected to the world,

not connected to their bodies,

not connected to other people,

not connected to natural processes,

not connected to an immanent, dynamic, concrete view of God,

not connected with the whimsical, intuitive, non-causal, playful, poetic in the universe.

I'm sure this is overstated. The truth here is that the predominant model, at least in western nations, has emphasized individual human nature but not the relational side of the self. With the loss of a focus on relationship, the self also lost connection with a sense of dependency on others, on nature, and on God. Things got pretty lonely. The model has led to structures and attitudes that are clearly dysfunctional for us and disastrous for the planet. **The model that is emerging is that of the relational self.**

3

Why the Health of the Environment Is a Spiritual Issue

Many people who do not think of themselves as religious exhibit a spiritual zeal about the environment.

Many who are very religious exhibit a similar zeal for different reasons. At least they think of them as different.

My intent in this chapter is to do two things: first, to explore why self-designated "non-religious" people nevertheless feel a deep commitment to the environment, and second, to suggest a new basis for environmental ethics, a basis rooted in relationships. The foundational relationships are those between God and nature, and between God and humanity.

Let's turn first to the relationship that many non-religious people do feel toward nature. We begin with the story of a rock climber:

> For my very first rock climbing experience, I chose a somewhat private spot, away from other climbers and on-lookers. After studying "the chimney," I focused all my energy on making it to the top. I climbed with intense determination, using whatever strength and skills I had to accomplish this challenging feat. By midway I was exhausted and anxious. I couldn't see what to do next—where to put my hands or feet. Growing increasingly more weary as I clung somewhat desperately to the rock, I made a move. It didn't work. I fell. There I was, dangling

midair above the rocky ground below, frightened but terribly relieved that the belay rope had held me. I knew I was safe. I took a look up at the climb that remained. I was determined to make it to the top. With renewed confidence and concentration, I finished the climb to the top.

On my second day of climbing, I rappelled down about 200 feet from the top of the Palisades at Lake Superior to just a few feet above the water level. I could see no one—not my belayer, not the other climbers, no one. I unhooked slowly from the rappel rope and took a deep cleansing breath. I looked all around me—really looked—and listened. I heard a cacophony of voices—birds, trickles of water on the rock before me, waves lapping against the rocks below. I closed my eyes and began to feel the rock with my hands—the cracks and crannies, the raised lichen and mosses, the almost imperceptible nubs that might provide a resting place for my fingers and toes when I began to climb.

At that moment I was bathed in serenity. I began to talk to the rock in an almost audible, child-like way, as if the rock were my friend. I felt an overwhelming sense of gratitude for what it offered me—a chance to know myself and the rock differently, to appreciate unforeseen miracles like the tiny flowers growing in the even tinier cracks in the rock's surface, and to come to know a sense of being in relationship with the natural environment. It felt as if the rock and I were silent conversational partners in a longstanding friendship.

I realized then that I had come to care about this cliff which was so different from me, so unmovable and invincible, independent and seemingly indifferent to my presence. I wanted to be with the rock as I climbed. Gone was the determination to conquer the rock, to forcefully impose my will on it; I wanted simply to work respectfully with the rock as I climbed. And as I climbed, that is what I felt. I felt myself caring for this rock and feeling thankful that climbing provided the opportunity for me to know it and myself in this way.[1]

What fascinates me about this story is the way it exemplifies a sense of spiritual zeal. It is a religious feeling that environmentalists frequently manifest. This story reminds me of a passage from John Muir. Once, upon returning to Yosemite from a trip, Muir reported that "all the rocks seem talkative and more lovable than ever. They are dear friends, and have warm blood gushing through their granite flesh, and I love them with a love intensified by a long and close relationship."[2] Neither the story nor Muir's passage are explicitly religious.[3] Yet both evoke a sense of the holy that can only be called "religious." They do this, not by recounting their encounters with more complex species—gorillas or chimpanzees, dogs, river otters, or giraffes—but with rocks.

My interest here lies not in attempting to **prove** the existence of God from our human experiences of nature, but rather in **describing** those experiences of the divine, or holy, or whatever it is we humans encounter in nature. We cannot assume to have captured all that an experience means by describing it. However, we may well learn something of nature's wisdom from Karen Warren's story or John Muir's experience of friendly rocks.

What is it that lies behind their spiritual zeal for the environment? Notice that both Warren's story and Muir's entry articulate their encounter with rocks. There is an interaction there between the human and the other-than-human. There is, in short, some relationship. In this relationship the rock plays an essential role as does the human subject.

1. *My first supposition is that spiritual zeal arises from the relationship people feel with nature*. This is not a human **domination** of nature, a relationship of **mastery over**, but of **relationship with** nature. So Warren reports that "I began to talk to the rock in an almost inaudible, child-like way, as if the rock were my friend." Muir also speaks of the rocks as "friends." Both identify the relationship as one that at first seems practically human.

On second thought, however, we are surprised to find that nonhuman, even inorganic entities can be relational partners with us. This feeling of being surprised arises from the historical view of humanity as separate from nature. We have in fact thought that humankind could only relate to, and only be substantially changed by, other human beings.

We know that we are influenced by other human beings. A rather sophisticated body of literature, and also our stock of everyday knowledge testifies to that. However, even though we may know that we are affected by nature as well, a far smaller body of literature and knowledge testifies to that influence. Our knowledge in this realm may be more intuitive than reflective. Even those who are sensitive to nature may overlook the way we are influenced by our relation to it.

Consider this passage from H. Richard Niebuhr which reflects the influence of George Herbert Mead, a leading social scientist of the 1920's and 30's:

> I do **not** wish to maintain that there is value in the self's relation to itself (or to its potential self) apart from its relations to others. . . . The theory of value I am seeking to present is through and through social; I know of no self-relatedness apart from other relatedness or self-alienation apart from the

other . . . the basis of this relational theory of value is not the relation of existence to essence, it is that of self to other.[4]

While I think Niebuhr's insight here is terribly important, I am at the same time struck with its anthropocentrism, its focus on the human. This is especially ironic in one who railed against anthropocentrism and included nature in his purview of concerns. What this demonstrates to me is the radical way human separation from nature gets carried in language and theory.

We can extend Niebuhr's relational theory of value to include the inorganic and organic world. Included are not only animate humans but all species as well. Going back to Warren and Muir's experiences we see that they felt themselves encountered by the rock; they felt rocks entering into friendship with them. There was a relationship established as much by the rock as by themselves. Though it would take far more argument to begin to establish this, I think we can describe their experience as "through and through social." There is "value in the self's relation to itself" precisely through "its relations to others," including the **whole** of the community of natural species and inorganic beings.

There are hundreds of images that express the human relationship with the earth that we feel in our bones. This is evident in Native American beliefs to an extent that may seem overwhelming to us. Luther Standing Bear exemplifies this relational consciousness:

So this land of the great plains is claimed by the Lakota as their very own. We are of the soil and the soil is of us. We love the birds and beasts that grew with us on this soil. They drank the same water as we did and breathed the same air. We are all one in nature. Believing so, there was in our hearts a great peace and a welling kindness for all living, growing things.[5]

A familiar image of the relationship pictures the earth as mother. Mother Earth communicates the relationship of having given birth to humanity or, more often, the sense that nature takes care of all her children. This image hearkens back to a succession of creation stories in the ancient Near Eastern world. There, especially in the earliest stories, it is the primal Mother or the Mother Goddess who creates the world.[6]

2. *Spiritual concern for the environment arises, secondly, because people sense a transcendence in the presence of nature*. They have a feeling of being in touch with a wider, more inclusive whole than is normally the case. This gives them/us a sense of identity with wider purposes. This sensation of transcendence is one that moves us beyond the routine, that transcends the moment and gives it a special quality. Notice that in Karen Warren's story the climber on her second day feels "bathed in serenity." John Muir at points speaks of the drive to know glacial forces: "The grandeur of these forces and their glorious results overpower me, and inhabit my whole being."[7]

Three aspects of these experiences are important. They seem first to come from beyond the person and almost strike the person with their palpable force. They are not manipulated or engineered. The person cannot cause them to happen. Second, they carry the person into a deeper field of meaning and fill the person with a holistic sensation. This meaning is intensely real and personal; it has residual effects in the everyday world and does influence the person's life there. However, there is simultaneously an inability to communicate that experience fully. This could be seen as having a mysterious or mystic quality. Finally the sense of transcendence, while arising from elsewhere, is integral to the person's relationship with nature. The transcendence is a force-in-relationship, not the quality of admiring a painting or a building or a sculpture from without. The human being is a part of the transcendence since they are implicated in it. Their own sense of relatedness to other forces is deepened by the encounter.

I believe that I am describing what could be called a religious experience. The word "religious" comes from the Latin *religar,* "to tie back" or "connect." Religion is a binding or tying-back experience; it indicates the bonds that exist in a way that goes beyond everyday fragmentation or sequencing. It reveals the nature of reality, of human relationships with wider forces—in this case, particularly with natural forces. The word seems to suggest primodiality as well. Religion ties us back to the basics.

In light of this it is interesting to note Freud's discussion of the source of religious sentiments. He investigates the notion that this source "is a feeling . . . a sensation of 'eternity,' a feeling as of something limitless, unbounded-as it were, 'oceanic.' "[8] This is the source of religious energy. On the grounds of this feeling alone, one may call oneself religious, even if one rejects every other belief, according to Freud. Though he does not call himself religious, he is able to acknowledge that others have this "oceanic" feeling. What is fascinating about this to me is Freud's choice of the natural image "oceanic" to describe the feeling and his identification of it as embodying a "oneness with the universe."[9]

3. *A third source of eco-spirituality arises from an awareness of the biosphere as a community.* Human beings have felt that their community was not restricted to other people. Some have observed the workings of an ecological system in its reciprocity and in the distinctive place each part has within that reciprocal whole. They have *felt* themselves a part of that biotic community, and that has generated a spiritual zeal for the environment.

Obviously this sense of **community** is related to the previous sources of eco-spirituality: the **relationship** men and
women feel with nature, and a sense of **transcendence** in the
presence of nature. All three of these have a large emotional
component. With this sense of community, however, there is
a considerable cognitive—even disciplinary—component.
This understanding of the cosmos and planet as a system of
interrelated parts forms the foundation of the science of
ecology.

However, without the **feelings** of respect and care for this
"system of interrelated parts," one would not call it "community" nor see oneself as part of it. Cognitive knowledge **suf-
fused** with emotional regard will produce religious commitment. This commitment can be seen in Karen Warren's
appreciation for "the almost imperceptible nubs that might
provide a resting place for my fingers and toes when I began to
climb." Or her sense of gratitude for the "unforeseen miracles
like the tiny flowers growing in the even tinier cracks in the
rock's surface." John Muir, though he argued for the intrinsic
value of every creature, also wrote: "In the making of every
animal the presence of every other animal has been
recognized."[10]

Aldo Leopold both feels the community of nature and
also uses the concept to express his land ethic. In many of his
essays, such as "Round River" and "Goose Music," Leopold
describes the interconnection of all life in community. The
starting point for any ethic is, he says, that "we can be ethical
only in relation to something we can see, feel, understand,
love, or otherwise have faith in."[11] The emotional or "faith"
commitment is key.

At another point in the same essay, Leopold indicates a
prerequisite of this ethic: "All ethics so far evolved rest upon a
single premise: that the individual is a member of a community of interdependent parts."[12] That recognition promotes

cooperation which will restrain competitive human instincts and ultimately promote survival. Leopold laments the fact that so many forces conspire to obscure the human being's community with land. What we need instead, he believes, is a land ethic which will enlarge the boundaries of community to include soils, water, plants, and animals. This leads naturally to Leopold's best known dictum:

> A thing is right when it tends to preserve the integrity, stability, and beauty of the biotic community. It is wrong when it tends otherwise.[13]

Leopold's essays articulate a love and respect for nature in its particular detail as well as in its universal scope. Through them Leopold is both informing and persuading us that we are members of the community of the land. An ingredient of this eco-spirituality is the realization that we human beings are part of the community. We belong here. We have a particular role to play, as do others, in the whole.

4. *There are a number of powerful emotions that are awakened through an encounter with nature*. These often give rise to a religious feeling about ecology, usually in conjunction with one or another of the three sources we have just examined.

Fear. Some feelings about nature are more ambiguous than those we have described thus far. When we hear reports of a ferocious hurricane or a California earthquake and see the power of those natural forces, we are apprehensive about the havoc they wreak. If we have ever been in the midst of such storms, we are especially afraid. Part of that fear is an awe, a respect, a self-diminution in the face of natural forces. In those instances we feel the hostility of the environment. We may even begin to understand the origins of the notion that nature is a hostile force that humankind has to control. Note that in

Warren's story, on the first day she saw chimney rock as something to be conquered. In short, the power of nature may sometimes be a fearful one, one that elicits images of nature as something to be domesticated. How fear, and the respect and awe-ingredient in fear, feed into religious sentiment is a matter for future discussion.

Friendship. It is unimaginable that fear by itself could be the sole source of religious zeal about the environment. Indeed, our exposition reveals that such religious fervor arises from a mixture of experiences, such as the ones we have discussed. One that is the opposite of fear is the feeling that the universe is human-friendly. Often this feeling is expressed through the image of "home." This world seems arranged to accommodate humanity; it is our home. It may, furthermore, appear friendly to other species as well. The environment is arranged to sustain and further life in many varieties. As a matter of fact, variety itself feeds into the friendliness of the world.

While far more attention could be paid to the sensation, wildness is a human attribution to nature which awakens feelings of both fear and friendliness. The experience of wilderness may evoke feelings of apprehension or fear at first. Fear may give way to friendliness as our initial apprehensions prove unfounded. When that happens, we may perceive the world as home for our and other species.

Beauty. Our human awareness of environmental beauty stimulates an eco-spirituality. The experience of beauty has the distinctive characteristic of engaging us, of attracting our positive attention. For example, a person seldom says, "I think that's beautiful, but I'm not attracted by it." Indeed, it is hard to imagine someone saying, "I suppose that is beautiful but I don't like it." The experience of beauty creates a relationship of some kind to the person, animal, or object found beautiful. The initial sensation of such an experience is not that of detachment of the observer from the observed. Rather, it is beauty that holds things together—intellectual, aesthetic, sexual, and natural beauty. It is an ingredient to health, not an occasional or voluntary choice.[14]

The intuition of beauty creates a relationship, a commitment that grounds moral concern. It leads to a love that issues forth in the desire to preserve natural beauty. That is why we find oil spills, deforestation, or abuse of animals repugnant.

Other feelings. There are any number of other strong emotions which could inspire a spirituality associated with the environment. I think of love, respect, and care, for example. These interrelate with sources of religiosity already mentioned, but seem to have some independent standing as well. Two that deserve some mention, however brief, are those of power and trustworthiness.

Confronted by the **power** of nature, human beings have discovered or established various religions on the basis of that experience. In Stoicism, for example, the unitary power of nature plays a central role. Still others find nature to be eminently **trustworthy**. They experience the environment to be dependable and find their trust to be realistic.

5. *The final source of eco-spirituality mentioned here arises from its association with other religions—most notably, deep ecology and feminism*. Deep ecology can be virtually a religion in its own right. The motivation of that movement includes the sources we have already described: relatedness, transcendence, community, and powerful emotions. The movement includes other religious elements as well—the association of believers with each other, for example. Community is especially important. Deep ecology is grounded in the religious vision arising from the experience and appreciation of community with other living things. Growing out of that vision are a set of eight principles for moral guidance.[15] Some of these are: the intrinsic value of all life; the preservation of the

richness and diversity of life-forms; a decrease in human population; and reducing wasteful life-styles.

Feminism is another movement which some have claimed is inevitably sensitive to environmental issues.[16] Feminism as a contemporary movement arose out of the experience of oppression. Women felt they were and still are systematically excluded from first-class citizenship. As a result of that experience it is easy to understand feminism's commitment to relational holism.

"The crisis that threatens the destruction of the earth is not only social, political, economic, and technological, but it is at root spiritual," writes Carol P. Christ.[17] What has been lost is the sense that earth is our true home and that we human beings are connected with all beings in the web of life. We need nothing less than a shift of consciousness: "a recovery of more ancient and traditional views that revere the connection of all beings in the web of life and a rethinking of the relation of humanity and divinity to nature."[18]

One of the first tenets of eco-feminism is the close relation between humanity and nature. Susan Griffin writes, "I know I am made from the earth, as my mother's hands were made from this earth, as her dreams . . . this paper, these hands, this tongue speaking, all that I know speaks to me through this earth and . . . you, you who are earth too. . . ."[19] Women have sometimes been assumed to be more closely related to nature because they were more physically determined. This association with the physical has been used to reinforce and legitimate the domination of women in the past.

Notice how Griffin **celebrates** the connection between nature and her physical self. This is a reformulation of the first order: a positive evaluation of the material connection between humanity and the world.[20] Feminist theory reverses the flow of the injurious dynamics we identified in chapter 2.

Another tenet of eco-feminism involves the reformulation of the relation of God to the environment. God becomes far more immanent in feminist theology than in mainstream contemporary theology. This underscores the intrinsic value of all life. Carol Christ quotes a passage from Alice Walker's *The Color Purple*, in which Shug is describing her vision of God:

> My first step from the old white man was trees. Then air. Then birds. Then other people. But one day when I was sitting quiet and feeling like a motherless child, which I was, it come to me: that feeling of being part of everything, not separate at all. I knew that if I cut a tree, my arm would bleed. And I laughed and I cried and I run all round the house. I knew just what it was. In fact, when it happen, you can't miss it. It sort of like you know what, she say, grinning and rubbing high up on my thigh. . . . I think it pisses God off if you walk by the color purple in a field and don't notice it. . . . Everything want to be loved. Us sing and dance, make faces and give flower bouquets, trying to be loved. You ever notice that trees do everything to git attention we do, except walk?[21]

Karen Warren builds her environmental ethic on an eco-feminist religious base. Her claim is that "any feminist theory and any environmental ethic which fails to take seriously the interconnection of women and nature is simply inadequate."[22]

To establish that claim Warren makes the following case. First, both sexism and humanocentrism are based on social domination—sexism, on the domination of women by men;

humanocentrism on the domination of the environment by humankind. Her second claim is that environmental ethics and feminist ethics both exhibit the same "boundary conditions." Those are the minimal conditions of an ethic. Both ethics are contextual; in both what matters are the relationships which enable parties to flourish. Both are open to a plurality of perspectives, ones that may change over time. They share a preference for moral choices that are inclusive of the perspectives of oppressed people and land. Finally, both center on the values of community, of care, of friendship, and on appropriate mutuality.[23] Thus both attempt to reverse the logic of domination. In summary, any environmental ethic which permits discrimination against women to continue, and any feminist ethic which permits discrimination against nature to continue, are quite simply inadequate.

Ecological Spirituality

We have located five common human experiences which are evoked by the environment. They constitute elements of a religion; if, in fact, they are not a religion themselves. The five are:

- people feel **related** to nature;
- often persons have a **sense of transcendence** in the presence of nature;
- people are aware of the biosphere as a **community**;
- human beings feel **powerful emotions** in the face of nature—**fear, friendship, beauty, power, trustworthiness**; and
- environmental awareness is associated with other religious commitments—**deep ecology** and **feminism**, in particular.

These are, of course, not the only sources of religious fervor surrounding the environment. However, they are so frequent a reaction to the environment that most people can identify with them. Those who feel them most intensely probably view the environment as a major source of their spirituality.

I trust that it has been clear that my intention has not been to prove the existence of God or some such. Rather, accepting that God is present in the world, **my intention has been to establish grounds for eco-spirituality**. It has been to describe those experiences that make for a religion of environmental appreciation **apart from explicit Christian categories**. This is emphatically different from assuming that God is not involved in the world.

What is important about the experiences we have uncovered is that they stand on their own. They arise out of human experience; they do not depend on prior theological commitments. Rather than depending on Christian sources which may not be persuasive to those who do not share that perspective, they are accessible to all. The truth and power of the experience does not depend on a **confessional** base.

What is evident **here** is the **relational** base of the experience. All of these experiences point toward a reality outside of the human, a transcendent reality resident in nature. In the next chapter we lay out the basic theological foundation. That foundation rests on experiences similar to those we have described here but also on biblical and theological understandings.

4

The Earth: God's Home, Our Home

In the previous chapter we spoke of how many people have begun to experience their relationship with the earth as a spiritual one. Christians should welcome these developments as part of God's revelation. The Christian faith is "the most avowedly materialist of religions" as William Temple affirmed on the basis of creation, incarnation, and spiritual indwelling.[1] It follows that the religious experience of those who are not explicitly Christian is something we should expect rather than find surprising or threatening. If we truly believe that God is present in the world, we should expect human beings to enjoy the beauty of creation.

We should avoid the temptation to force those who do not identify themselves as Christian to acknowledge God as the author of the beauty they experience. The call of the Christian is to affirm that the earth is God's without manipulating others. Our evangelism is **for the sake of others, out of a desire for their delight and well-being,** not to reinforce our own beliefs. In fact, God has often enriched the lives and understandings of the Christian community through those who do not acknowledge the same formal confession of faith. Perhaps this is one of those times.

We need to say more, however. We need to listen to feminists, to deep ecologists, and to others because the Spirit of God may be speaking to us through them. God might be moving through them in the same dynamic way God spoke through the prophets, through the Hebrew scriptures, through Paul, John, and Luke. It is the same dynamism found in the tradition and theology of the living church. Revelation is continuous.

The Christian community maintains that God speaks through scripture and uses scripture as the canon, the standard for measuring ongoing revelation. The message we are receiving from some of the groups mentioned is, in general, consistent with the word of God. This is no time for the environmentally concerned to engage in intramural squabbles. At the same time, each religious community and movement should use its unique perspectives to develop engaging, truthful insights which promote care for the earth.

There are two reasons for the Christian community to articulate a faithful theology of the environment: one is the mandate to obey God's will that we care for the earth. The other is the perspective developed by the distinctive truths of the Christian faith. The Hebrew and early church scriptures can speak with power to our environmental quandry. They can assist us in gaining insight on our place in the environment and our responsibility in relation to it.

This chapter will lay the foundation of a theology which addresses the current situation (as interpreted in chapters 2 and 3) from the viewpoint of the Bible and theology. Frankly, the Christian love of the earth is an underdeveloped tradition. We will retrieve this tradition here and in the remaining chapters of this book.

The Metaphor of Home

Thinking of the earth as home is one way of picking up many of the biblical themes. The scriptures have much to say about the world, too much to compress into one image or metaphor.[2] It is, nevertheless, part of our human constitution that we think best with the use of images. Good images make for good thinking. Home is one such image.

To say that the earth is our home goes against many of the attitudes that have brought us to our current situation. Furthermore, that image even goes against many popular Christian conceptions. My contention, to the contrary, is that the image of earth as home is a fruitful way to express many Christian themes and understandings. Surely it is more biblical than an other-worldly, spiritualized interpretation of the Christian life. An other-worldly emphasis may be more subtle today than it was when people used to sing, "This world is not my home, I'm only passing through." However, this attitude may evidence itself in such theological emphases as: disembodiment or fear of physicality; an individualized piety of devotion; a theoretical avoidance of political or economic life; or concentration on narrowly personal categories.

Contrary to the theological themes and secular attitudes we have been looking at, the image of the earth as home suggests: embodiment in a particular location; a corporate life of faithful activity; the expectation and interpretation of political and economic features; and interpersonal and transpersonal dimensions interpenetrating the personal.

The reasons which explain our present environmental dilemma (chapter 2) are related to the biblical themes which emphasize otherworldliness. For example, our sense that we lack knowledge and power—the first reason—stems at least partly from individualism and the avoidance of political or economic life. Similarly, the dominant values of our economic system which encourage disregard for the environment (reason two) arise from economic life and from concentrating on the narrowly personal dimension of Christianity. Considering the other three root sources of environmental disrespect we could show similar interconnections. There is a linkage between dominant theological themes which emphasize otherworldliness and the wholly secular reasons we identified in chapter 2 as underlying our current situation.

What I am asserting is that theological themes and secular cultural attitudes often display similar emphases. These themes reinforce each other and perpetuate the status quo. Ideas from whatever source (religious, scientific, artistic) shape cultural attitudes and those attitudes in turn shape behaviors which, of course, shape ideas as well. To change this cycle we must intervene at some point. My suggestion is that we intervene at the point of images and ideas which shape attitudes and behavior.

Biblical Themes

God's Home. We can understand that the earth is God's home in light of ecological interpretations of two major biblical concerns: redemption and creation. Let us consider redemption first.

Redemption. How many times have we heard "God so loved the world that he gave his only Son, . . . that the world might be saved through him" (Jn 3:16, 17)? When we read or hear that, I suspect we think that the world that God loved and saved includes only people. We think that the redemption achieved by Christ extends only to human beings.

In the Old Testament, as well as the New, God is presented as renewing the whole created order. When Jeremiah asks, "How long will the land mourn, and the grass . . . wither?" (12:4; see also Isa 24:4–6, Hos 4:3, Isa 5:8), he is asking about the whole earth. The answer that comes is Yahweh's response of mercy to the degradation of earth and the restoration of human beings. The promise is that God will renew the earth. (Ps 104:30). Through the series of covenants set up with humankind, God expresses the intention to redeem the cosmos. The Noahic covenant is especially poignant in this regard, as the partners in the covenant are God, Noah and his family, and "every living creature that is with you, the birds, the cattle, and every beast." (Gen 9:10) This covenant with the earth (Gen 9:13) underscores God's love and care for her home. (See also Hos 2:18–22, Isa 62:4, 55:12, 65:17.)

Building on the covenant promises which express God's overriding care, the New Testament portrays Jesus Christ as the reconciler. The reconciliation achieved by Jesus Christ extends to the whole creation, "For in him the fullness of God was pleased to dwell, and through him to reconcile all things . . ." (Col 1:19–20).

The whole creation, as Paul portrays it, eagerly awaits its full transformation. "The creation itself is to share in the freedom, in the glorious and undying goodness, of the children of God" (Rom 8:19–21). We and the earth have entered into the renewal achieved by Jesus Christ. **The earth itself is the object of God's redemption, as are human beings**.

Creation. Starting with the redemption of the earth as revealed in the incarnation gives us a different slant on the biblical notion of creation. Creation becomes less a static **fait accompli** completed in the first two chapters of Genesis than a continuing process linked with redemption.

The linkage is clear in the "hymn to creation" of Colossians 1:15. There Jesus Christ is "the image of the invisible God, the first-born of all creation; for in him all things were created, in heaven and on earth, visible and invisible. . . ." The idea is that Jesus Christ joined God the creator at the time of creation. Genesis 1:2 reveals that the Spirit was present then as well, "moving over the face of the waters."

Current studies are emphasizing the **continuing** creativity and sustenance of God.[3] This emphasis opens onto a dynamic conception of God and a sense that we are or can be a part of that continuing creation. The Psalms and Job 38–39 convey one aspect of this; namely, God's continuing delight in creation. God delights in sea creatures, mountain goats, and whirlwinds. Another aspect is God's indwelling creation which Jurgen Moltmann has identified with the Holy Spirit, *God in Creation.*[4] (Rom 8:16; Jn 3:5, 2 Cor 1:22, 5:5; Eph 1:14, 1 Cor 6:13–20; 1 Cor 12.)

Many have called attention to the goodness of creation, as certified by God's seeing "everything that he had made, and behold, it was very good" (Gen 1:31). Fewer have noted the delight that Jesus takes in the earth. Often we dismiss the outside settings and the natural objects and images in the parables of the gospels as mere vehicles rather than part of the content of Jesus' teaching. I believe this to be due to our own truncated understanding, a truncation growing out of our anti-natural bias in religion. We seem to feel a need to abstract spiritual and religious meaning out of its concrete occurrence and leave the material hull behind. I believe this is what Whitehead described as the first step in the fallacy of misplaced concreteness (which is to identify the abstracted as the real).

Jesus certainly was at home on this earth. Could it be that Jesus' being at home, being fully human, was part of the divine revelation? A revelation that God is at home on earth? On what basis would one exclude that sense of affection for the earth from being part of the incarnate revelation? That we ignore Jesus' example of affection and prefer the written word indicates our selective vision.[5]

In line with this, the world of science in many ways reveals a divinely governed ecological balance in the environment. Because Christians and Jews perceive creation as emanating from God, the world when interpreted "in piety" offers "signs of the power and presence of God."[6] From within the faith Christians see science as a theological discipline for interpreting God's ordering of the world. The wisdom literature of the Bible perceives God's wisdom as "naturally" occurring for the same reason. (See Prov 3:19–20, passim; Job 12:10; 1 Kings 4:33; Eccl; Ps 8, 19, 104, 148.) God has become **very**

much at home in this world when consequences flow from violations of God's laws.[7] God's laws include both moral and natural ones. Thus instances of ecological destruction can be seen as violations of God's and science's laws. Similarly, the Catholic notion of the cosmos coming from and returning to God emphasizes God's sovereignty and the continuity of divine care.

The rich pastoral imagery of the Bible bespeaks a people who find God's activity in nature and in natural regularities. A frequent instance of such pastoral imagery speaks of God's care for her earth. God's care for sparrows, ravens, and birds in general, as Jesus reminds us, is an assurance of God's greater care for humans. In the rush to human assurance we should not miss God's independent and real concern for the wild birds (Mt 6:26; 19:29–30; Lk 12:6–7, 24). Not only do human beings and ravens receive their food and their being from God, so also do lions and rock badgers.[8]

We can now unequivocally affirm that God does indeed dwell on earth. This is God's home. In saying that we do want to avoid two pitfalls. The first is claiming that God is contained by the earth, is limited to the earth as home. We need to be clear that calling the earth God's home is not a comprehensive statement: God may have many homes. We want to avoid any depreciation of God. It is terribly illuminating that we have no trouble speaking of God as being active in history and culture, but much greater difficulty understanding God to be active in nature and continuing creation. The intent of this book is to offer a counterbalance to the depreciation of God inherent in reading God out of nature and creativity. At the same time seeing the earth as a divine ecology will make for the flourishing of all life in God. A theocentric focus is vital to the well-being of creation.

The second trap is exclusivism—the notion that home

consists only of human beings. Perhaps even only of human beings who resemble us in race, income level, gender, ethnicity, education, age or cleanliness. The use of the metaphor "home" in reference to the earth can become anthropocentric,[9] or even ethnocentric. Humankind becomes the only species. Perhaps this is due to the individualizing, spiritualizing tendency of our culture or perhaps to a persistent human sinfulness. There is a real danger that we will come to consider the earth as "home for us alone," rather than having its own independent value for God as God's home. The metaphor of the earth as God's home tries to structure out anthropocentrism, as well as racist or other exclusivist reduction of the common good to "good for us." Whenever the good becomes good only for high **or** low income people, for only black **or** red **or** brown, then the earth is no longer God's home or ours. The earth is really our corporate home.

Human Home. Taking a theocentric perspective has led us to consider the biblical image of the earth as God's home. We turn now to what those and other themes say about the earth as home for humankind. To do so, we will first point to different elements of the meaning of "home" and then ask how the Bible presents earth as home.[10]

The most important feature of a home is that it is **our place, a place where our identity finds its fullest range of expression**. It is the place where we are most ourselves. "Be it ever so humble, there's no place like home" because we locate ourselves there. We treasure our homes beyond their monetary value because they are an important part of ourselves.

One element that commends the base metaphor of the earth as God's home is that it signals a series of relationships. It is a connectional metaphor which is just what we need to remedy a fragmentary view of our life. The tendency to identify God with history and culture is more susceptible to nationalism and racism than is the conception of God as involved with nature and creation.[11] One of the relationships constituting our identity is the relationship with God.

Homeplace. The Bible is replete with images of how God enters into relationship with humankind. We will focus on one tradition which emphasizes how God entered into relationship through the earth—the blessing tradition, the gift tradition. This tradition emphasizes the continuous ways that God has blessed, is blessing, and will bless humankind. In its emphasis on the normal routine structures of life, it is in continuity with the creation and redemption themes. It commends the multiple ways that God acts through nature and continuing creation every day. This is not, however, the dominant school of biblical interpretation.

The dominant school in this century, the **Heilsgeschichte**, or salvation history school, highlights the mighty acts of God in saving and preserving a chosen people. Thus it stresses the series of covenants between God and the Hebrew peoples, and the sin-salvation cycle of **history**.[12] Though the content can differ from one interpreter to another, all those who emphasize the biblical motifs of covenant, deliverance and exodus emphasize the God who acts in **history** and **culture**. What is needed to round out these schools of thought is an interpretation which includes nature and creation–the blessing tradition.

Claus Westermann describes blessing in terms of the gradual processes of growing, maturing, and fading. "The Old Testament does not just report a series of events which consist of the great acts of God. The intervals are also part of it."[13] The Deuteronomic tradition of the gift of land and the blessing that accompanies the land are part of this blessing tradition. The promise of land, the efforts of the people, and the regular persisting features of the earth are the bedrock of our lives. They are the background features which enable all life. They give us so much support that we take them for granted until God's good gifts of earth, air, and water are threatened. The goodness of the incarnation reinforces the giftedness of our lives by Jesus Christ and the earth.

One of the implications of the blessing tradition is that God has so arranged the creation that our lives bloom in God's home. This is one connotation of the language of the "orders of creation" (Luther, Brunner, etc.). Gustafson has been quite explicit about the regularized patterns of existence that characterize our earth, and enable life to flourish.[14] The earth is home to human beings because God designed the world so it would be our place.

Shared. While God designs the earth to be our place—the source of our identity and the structure which enables our life, it is a home that we share. Sometimes we speak of having a "homeplace" which may or may not be our present residence. What we connote by that term is the place most formative of our identity. That place is, I suspect, seldom unpopulated. **Home is shared**. We speak of home as a dwelling which has emotionally engaged us because of the relationships which happen there—the good times we have, the significant others we meet, the shaping events that we undergo with others. This includes people primarily, but it is also shared with pets and flowers and gardens and home improvements we make there. The relationships we share lend a distinctive ambience to the place; they color it in certain ways. We value the place because of the events we experience with others there. At a certain point the place and the relationships merge; to think of one evokes the other.

Certainly our tradition presents a picture of a **shared** home. The second great commandment enjoins us to treat our neighbor as we do ourselves (Mt 22:39; Mt 19:19; Lev 19:18). Throughout the canon it is clear that we were not created to live alone. Indeed, the punishment for the greedy who "join house to house, who add field to field" is that they "are made to dwell alone in the midst of the land" (Isa 55:8). The fact that we share the earth with other people is so central to the biblical description that it seems axiomatic.

What is also central but far less recognized is that we share the earth with many other creatures. Both creation stories tell us that human beings are to share the earth (Gen 1:28, 2:15). The law is full of references to domestic livestock and how they are to be treated (Dt 25:4; 1 Cor 9:9–10; Ex 20:17; Mt 12:11; Lk 14:5). Similarly the land itself is shared—it has an independent value which we are to respect (Lev 25:1–7).

Place of Caring. Closely related to the fact that home is a shared place is the ideal that it be a place of caring. **Home is the place where we care for others and others care for us**. One current connotation of "home" is that it is a refuge, a haven from the stress of public life. Whether we deplore or applaud this privatization of home, the impression is that home is a refueling station, a place where one finds strength and renewal. Beverly Harrison speaks of "our enabling each other into being."[15] By this she points to the physical and emotional ways that we shape and are shaped by others. We simply would not **be** without the care of others, nor they without us. That claim is a literal and theological one; we could not **be** without care. Home is a place where creating, re-creating, and healing can happen. That, at least, is the ideal.

Scripture strongly asserts that it is not enough to share the earth if that means a cold, legalistic coexistence. That is no longer possible. Our sharing is to take the form of caring, and that caring extends both to other human beings and to animals and all living things. The Jubilee commandment (Lev 25; Dt 19:14; Prov 23:10–11; Mic 2:1–5) links care for land and care for people. Similarly sabbath rest should be extended not only to servant and family members but also to cattle and strangers (Ex 20:8–11). The law code and the prophets have much to say about how earth should be shared with others and cared for.

The care for animals can illustrate this. We have cited the care for domestic livestock so often exhibited in law (Ex 23:4–5, 12; Dt 22:1–4; Dt 5:14, 22:10, 25:4; Lev 19:19). When animals are used by human beings, they are to be used carefully. When they are sacrificed or even killed outside the ritual of sacrifice, that is to be done in a sacred, reverent spirit (Dt 12:15, 21; Acts 10:13, 11:7). George Frear claims that the primal state in Genesis envisions a vegetarian world; God gives humans vegetation to eat. Only later, with the Fall, do humans get permission from God to eat animals. (Gen 9:2–3). This concern for animals is also communicated through the image of the peaceable kingdom, the home par excellence, where wolf and lamb, leopard and kid, calf and lion will all lie down together (Isa 11:6–9, 65:25).

A Place of Conflict. Sometimes the many expectations that get placed on home and family are not met. Homes break down under the weight of unmet expectations. Thus, another characteristic of homes is that they are **one of the places prone to conflict** in our society. The diversity of often-conflicting needs and desires erupt in ways that are destructive. If conflicts do not get handled satisfactorily, then one's home breaks up. This may be the result of a divorce, or it may be that one's former home loses its emotional quality and becomes more or less a shell.

Since the earth is our home, we can expect to find the full array of sins and of justice there that we know from our personal home life. Indeed, the radical nature of sin has become rooted in the land. However, structures of care have likewise protected our home from greater degradation.

Scripture is realistically open-eyed about the presence of sin in our human actions. So, 2 Chronicles 6:36: "There is no [man] who does not sin," or Paul in Romans 3:23: "We have all sinned and fall short of the glory of God." There is apparently an inherent conflict between our human motives and desires and those of God (Jas 4:4). The temptation of Jesus in the wilderness (Mt 4:1–11) is a graphic example of this conflict. The mention of the devil is almost always a signal of this conflict (Jn 6:70; Eph 4:27; Heb 2:14; 1 Peter 5:8; Rev 12:9).

To assist us in resisting evil and sinfulness, God gives the law to lead people into the ways of righteousness and justice. Thus, the laws of agricultural recompense for injuries (Ex 21:28–22:15), the gleaning laws (Dt 23:24–25, 24:21–22) and other ecological laws (Ex 23:4–5; Lev 19:19; Dt 22:6–7, Dt 20:19–20) all point to the way of justice.

The cycle of promise of land, realization of promise, then violation of law, exile from land, and subsequent restoration of land takes place several times in Old Testament history. So Yahweh, in both Leviticus and Deuteronomy, promises that "If you live according to my laws, if you keep my commandments and put them into practice, I shall give you the rain you need at the right time; the soil will yield its produce and the trees of the countryside their fruit . . ." (Lev 26:3–4ff.; cf. also Dt 8). When the people violate these laws, however, God's judgment is swift, but also merciful. In a particularly vivid passage, Yahweh speaks of the people Israel:

> And now they sin more and more . . .
> Therefore they shall be like the morning mist . . .
> like the chaff that swirls from the threshing floor . . .
> I am the Lord your God . . .
> It was I who knew you in the wilderness,
>   in the land of drought:
> but when they had fed to the full . . .
>   they forgot me.
> So I will be to them like a lion
>   like a leopard I will lurk beside the way.

> I will fall upon them like a bear
> robbed of her cubs . . .
>
> (Hosea 13:2–8ff)

In Hosea 14 the Lord offers restoration in similar terms:

> I will be as the dew to Israel;
> he shall blossom as the lily,
> he shall strike root as the poplar;
> his shoots shall spread out . . .
> They shall return and dwell beneath my shadow,
> they shall flourish as a garden;
> they shall blossom as the vine . . .
>
> (Hosea 14:5–7ff)

Abused land, like fallen people, may yet hope for liberation, for

> Desert [the Lord] changes into standing pools,
> and parched land into springs of water.
> There [God] gives the hungry a home . . . they reap a
> fruitful harvest.
> God blesses them and their numbers increase . . .
>
> (Psalm 107:35–38)

The tone of this psalm and especially verse 41a, "But [God] raises up the needy out of affliction," and 40a, "[God] pours contempt upon princes," remind me of the Magnificat:

> [God] has put down the mighty from their thrones,
> and exalted those of low degree;
> [God] has filled the hungry with good things,
> and the rich [God] has sent empty away.
>
> (Luke 1:52, 53)

Our home, the earth, gives evidence of human sinfulness and injustice.[16] BUT it also manifests the possibility of justice and righteousness. Humankind can insensitively abuse its home for private, individual gain, or it can live up to God's intentions for the land.

There is grace. The reality of God's grace, both in deliverance and in everyday blessing, is real. Humankind has the chance of drawing on and living out that grace. The possibility of sin and abuse is also real. We can operate at cross-purposes with grace. Finally, however, we know there will be a "new heaven **and a new earth**" (Rev 21:1), God will restore creation, and there will be the cosmic unity spoken of as **shalom**, the peace of God.

Home for Animals, Plants, Water, and Land. Since we have often seen the earth as unrelated to us, I have emphasized that part of the Christian tradition that affirms that the earth is our human home. The earth is also God's home. The animals, plants, rivers, and soil have significance to God independently of their value to humankind.

Throughout this chapter I have shown that it is all of creation that is home. Our tradition—from biblical laws specifying how we are to cherish the land and animals, to the examples of St. Francis, Albert Schweitzer and Thomas Berry—asserts that this earth is home for all creatures great and small. It is home for plants, for rocks, for bodies of water, and for the soil that teems with life.

The earth is arranged to satisfy the needs and delights of all beings. Many in the Catholic tradition have celebrated the relationships that God established with creation and also those that God built into the fabric of life—those between animals and plants, between the land and human beings, between water and life, and between human beings. All these beings have value in themselves and also in relationship.

All of these beings and ourselves are **at home** in the sense that we exist in ourselves and in relationship. The earth is not an external home; **we are part of the home**. We are part of the earth. The whole web of life that is the earth cannot be externalized from us. We are all part of God's home; we constitute nature.

We are not at home; we are home! The rest of this book will be an exploration of what it means to be part of God's home.

5

Being Ourselves:
The Human-Nature Relationship

We come now to the most distinctive aspect of this book. What I want to push you to consider is this:

You are an integral part of the natural world.

Perhaps that could be expressed even more simply:

You are natural.

Do you identify more with your mind than your body? If so, then you probably see yourself as more historical than natural.

Of course that last question is a rather stupid one because we identify our selves both with our minds and our bodies. Nevertheless, there are profound roots to our greater identification with our minds and our historical features. Those associations need to be questioned so we may correctly begin to see ourselves as integrated historical-natural beings who are in relation to the whole biosphere.[1]

Being Natural

I see this as terribly important for several reasons, some of which have already been touched on in previous chapters.

In chapter 2 one of the prominent reasons we cited as contributing to environmental negligence was that human beings see
themselves as **not essentially part of** nature. Rather we see
ourselves as **apart from** nature. Put very bluntly, what this
means is that men, women, and children do not understand
that it is in their self-interest to look after their home. They
think that ultimately their environment doesn't really matter.

Furthermore this perception underlies literally every one
of the other reasons for our cavalier attitude toward the earth.
For example, the fact that nature has been treated as a secondary concern theologically derives from our view that God
doesn't take nature very seriously, despite the biblical evidence to the contrary. Christians maintain that God does take
humankind very, very seriously, however. **That** illustrates **the
theological misconception that we human beings are not natural**. If human beings **were** considered natural, Christian theology would soon elevate God's view of nature. A little cynical?
Maybe. True? Most likely.

On the other hand, those who exhibit a religious zeal for
the natural world do so because they experience a relationship
with nature. Chapter 3 indicated some of those experiences—
a sense of unity with the world of nature, of transcendence in
the encounter with nature, of beauty, and of trust. What is
common to all those experiences is that in them the human
being feels a relationship with that part of nature which lies
outside themselves. One might even call it a kinship. They see
themselves as at least somewhat natural. What I want to emphasize in this regard is that human beings are not the same as
the rest of natural beings, any more than a rabbit is a marigold
or a goldfinch is a maple. All these beings are related. They are
all natural. They are also all different, as we are.

The Christian tradition in Bible and theology, as we explored it, also emphasizes that the earth is God's home, as well
as ours and animals'. It described human beings as thoroughly

natural and spiritual. It is vital to note that being natural and being spiritual are not opposites but are in fact dimensions of the human creature. How could men and women experience religious wonder, for example, except through the body? Indeed, there is a proud mystic tradition in theology which is not at all bashful about its view that natural embodiment and spirituality interpenetrate. Among its representatives are St. Irenaeus, Hildegarde of Bingen, and Meister Eckhart.[2] If the earth is our home then we are native to it, natural. If we claim that the earth is also God's home, then we are claiming that the natural is both good and spiritual. "The earth is full of the glory of God."

What happens when we forget that we are natural beings is that we begin to lose sight of the way in which we are limited. We are tempted to step out of the circle of nature and pretend that we are more important than other natural beings. This becomes a temptation to use, to dominate, and to abuse the earth as though it were home only to us. It is to lose sight of the way our limited embodiment is related to others. Much of the joy in our lives arises from such relatedness. Without a sense of limitations, we can ignore the way our naturalness enables us to enjoy life.

My claim is that we human beings are natural. I have tried to state why this matters as much as it does. Because it does the bulk of this chapter will be devoted to establishing that human beings are natural. We will then begin to consider just what the relationship between human beings and nature involves morally.

By this time surely you have wondered how it is that, if we are natural beings, we could have ignored that aspect of ourselves. Richard Lang offers one answer. Basically he says that our living in the world, our "dwelling" here is **so** natural that we can barely stand far enough back from it to think about that:

A meditation upon human dwelling reveals our primal embodied existence, our being-in-the-world. The notion of dwelling is the most taken-for-granted aspect of human existence. For this very reason [it] is the most obscure problem upon which we may reflect.... Contemplating the notion of inhabiting discloses our primitive alliance with the world and thereby unsettles the natural embeddedness and forgetfulness of human existence.[3]

Thinking about the fact that we are naturally physical and embodied reveals the alliance human beings have with the physical world. Reflecting on ourselves reveals **our** niche in the world. We have an alliance with others—beings upon which we depend and others who depend on us. Thinking about our interdependence with them discloses how much we are embedded in nature, even to the point of forgetfulness.

This is the point I want to make most vigorously, so vigorously in fact that it is incorporated in the title of this book: **We are so natural that it is false to say even that we are at home on earth. Rather, we are home; we constitute home.** That requires explanation, of course.

Knowing Ourselves

Martin Heidegger gave a lecture in 1951 addressing, in part, the severe housing shortage in post-World War II Germany.[4] For Heidegger the housing shortage was symptomatic of a far more fundamental problem—the homelessness of modern humanity. By this he meant the rootlessness of our way of life and even **psyches**. "Our modern era," echoes David Seamon, "cultivates journey, horizon, and reach often at the expense of dwelling, centers and homes."[5] Achievement,

travel, and innovation seem more essential to us than depend-
ability, neighborhood, and tradition. Though our era values
the first set of terms far more than the latter, both are integral
parts of human life.

A far-reaching challenge grows out of this tendency. Our
rootlessness may arise from not understanding who we are.
"We are not at home because we no longer understand who
we are," writes Michael Zimmerman. "One can live peace-
fully or dwell appropriately only if one knows, at some profound level, who one really is."[6] In our terms, to be at home
we need to know who we are. Obviously the way we define
ourselves is also significant to the theological claims that we
make. It is significant in determining where we should place
our time and energies. How we see ourselves influences what
we buy, what we believe, how we act, and how we relate to
others.

Let me offer a concrete and simple example. If we believe
that people are basically trustworthy, then we will act very
differently than we would if we believed them to be hostile. If
we believe people to be antagonistic at base, then we might
prepare to protect ourselves against them or to make preemp-
tive strikes on them. Extending the example to corporate entities, such as national governments, you can imagine the dif-
ferences such corporate beliefs might make in international
relations.

My point is that assumptions about who human beings
are influence our conduct. Misassumptions can lead to destructive and dangerous results. The assumptions we make
about ourselves are no different. Here the misassumption we
will focus on is that we exist apart from or above nature, that
we are not natural.

Many consequences flow from that misassumption. Consider the quantity of waste we produce. The root problem here
is that we think we can avoid the consequences of what we do,

that we exist apart from the "disposable" waste we produce. The truth is that we Americans, all of us, writes Wendell Berry,

> have become a kind of human trash, living our lives in the midst of a ubiquitous damned mess of which we are at once the victims and the perpetrators. . . . Our waste problem . . . is the fault of an economy that is wasteful from top to bottom—a symbiosis of an unlimited greed at the top and a lazy, passive, and self-indulgent consumptiveness at the bottom—and all of us are involved in it. If we wish to correct this economy, we must be careful to understand and to demonstrate how much waste of human life is involved in our waste of the material goods of Creation.[7]

The problem of waste is a powerful example because it shows just how everyday, routine, and all-pervasive the fallout from our perceived separation from nature is. We think that we can avoid the natural consequences of what we naturally do— eat, drink, defecate, shelter ourselves, etc. How can we reverse this?

First, however, I have to indicate just how deep this failure to understand ourselves is. A major philosophical school of this century, existentialism, often spoke of "homelessness," of "being thrown into an alien universe." Existentialism essentially wrote off nature. It saw humankind as existing in essential non-relation to nature. Existentialism maintained a metaphysical dualism between the human sphere and the sphere of nature. In it nature is viewed as lacking value, purpose, or ends. In such a world "the self is thrown back entirely upon itself in quest for meaning and value. Meaning is no longer found but is 'conferred.' Values are no longer beheld in the vision of objective reality [such as nature provides] but are posited as feats of valuation."[8]

Insofar as existentialism has an impact on theology it encourages contemporary thought to focus only on divine and human **agency** in history. "Christocentric, eschatological, historicist, and personalist concentrations have marked dominant movements in modern Protestant and Catholic theology alike."[9] Consequently, the doctrine of creation, with its stress on God's action in nature and on humanity's **rootedness** in nature, has too often been relegated to the shadows.

Indeed. The first step toward reversing this blindness about who we are is to understand that we are natural. We are not only the agents and actors who make history and who build things, we are also the creatures who live in nature and who enjoy life. We live out both history and nature. We **are** a natural history, a historical nature.

How can we make this case? What evidence could persuade us that we are natural? My perspective is that the Gordian knot that must be severed is our continuing to think of ourselves as mind separated from body. That bit of philosophical distinction is written deep into our psyches. It is the dichotomy associated with nature and history, but also with space and time. Perhaps the first step is to identify the hidden aspect of ourselves. Space, which is physical and therefore natural, can be understood as part of our human constitution. I have used the term "spatiality" to indicate how human beings are physical and natural.

It is human beings' spatiality that has been forgotten until recently.[10] The reasons why it was forgotten have to do with the greater emphasis modernity places on human freedom, on the mind, and on achievement than it does on human embeddedness, on the body, and on enjoying. This fits with what we have seen to be the dominant emphases in our culture. Spatiality reminds us that we are limited and are also at home. Thus it is important to a theology of the environment that we recover this aspect of ourselves. Physical spatiality is a feature that human beings share with other natural beings. Thus, it can help us recover an understanding of how we are related to nature, how we are natural.

What I propose is to use this aspect of ourselves to indicate that we are irrevocably physical even in those areas which we have most often dissociated from the spatial, natural aspects of ourselves: our minds, our relationships, and our spiritual lives. Those three correspond to three aspects of our spatial being: embodiment, sociality, and symbolization.[11]

Embodiment

To my mind the strongest evidence that we are natural comes from the realm of biology. Over and over scientists are discovering that those human functions which are dualistically associated only with the mind involve the body as an ineradicable partner. Evidence from the study of brain chemistry, physiological psychology, and psychosomatic medicine reveals that we are natural, but this does not threaten our spirituality.[12] Rather, it helps us reconceptualize spirituality as natural. That is getting ahead of our story, however. At present we are going to track down the notion of disembodiment and demonstrate that even the most dualistically-defined areas of mind are material and physical.

An analysis of embodiment will show that our organic constitution is integral to the human search for meaning and essential to sociality. Few examples are as powerful in showing just how interrelated body and mind are as brain chemistry. So-called "higher" brain functions that we associate with the human mind are physiologically dependent.

The brain is primarily made up of nerve cells called neurons. Information from other parts of the body travels to the brain along thousands of nerve pathways that make up the body's nervous system. Neurons process and convey this information through nerve impulses and chemical transmissions. Regulation of body functions, performance of voluntary and involuntary motor activities, and intellectual skills such as reasoning, analysis and language activity are all dependent upon the work of these tiny cells.[13]

The dependency of higher brain functions on the physical activity of the brain is evident in cases of chemical imbalance or malfunction, such as schizophrenia. Severe schizophrenia is characterized by disordered thought, delusions, and auditory hallucinations. Recent studies suggest that schizophrenia is linked to a sensitivity to the chemical transmitter dopamine. Use of antipsychotic drugs to block dopamine receptors often relieves the symptoms.[14]

The physicality of rational thought is also attested to when certain areas of the brain have been damaged or have undergone radical surgical procedures. Studies of the right and left hemispheres of the brain have shown that, in most people, the left hemisphere strongly connects to language ability, while damage to the right hemisphere affects spatial awareness, musical ability, recognition of other people and awareness of one's own body.[15]

All voluntary acts, as well as many involuntary ones, are the result of basic brain processes. For example, if a person standing in the street suddenly spies an oncoming car, sensory impulses from his eyes are relayed to other cells of the cerebral cortex and these nerve cells then transmit impulses to the muscles of the legs, making him step back onto the curb in time to let the car pass by. Although this entire process may take only a few seconds, it involves several different nerve pathways and many different nerve cells.[16]

Similar processes enable us to think abstractly, to connect different truths. We react to stimuli of all kinds—heat, reading, seeing a friend—with the aid of brain biochemistry. Brain wave patterns are also affected by various chemical and physiological changes in the body. If the brain's blood supply is interrupted even for only 15 seconds, the EEG fails rapidly in amplitude due to the cells' lack of oxygen. Our internal processes, then, are physical and natural. As we saw earlier our very breathing connects us with the environment that lies beyond us. The CO_2 we exhale nurtures plant life just as the oxygen plants exhale nourishes us. Together we constitute a symbiotic relationship which deeply embeds us in nature.

Sociality

Sometimes we assume that our capacity for relationships with other human beings sets us apart from the rest of nature. We think this is not natural; indeed, sometimes we have assumed it establishes our superiority. However, two arguments indicate how it is that our sociality is very much a physical and natural feature of our lives. The first builds on the fact that we are physical beings; the second considers the sociality of animals—hogs in particular.

What led us into a brief tour of brain processes was the desire to establish the fact that human beings are natural. The clearest evidence of that is our physicality, a property we share with other natural beings. According to Stephen Toulmin and June Goodfield, modern physics understands matter as atoms running from subatomic wavicles to viruses to human beings, **but all composed of the same basic material.**[17]

Furthermore, the material constitution that we share is dynamic. Atoms are no longer understood as building blocks but as dynamic units "defined by characteristic patterns of energy and activity."[18] Matter is not inert, nor are our bodies.

They are not merely vehicles; they live in and through interaction with the environment. They are a component of the environment in relation to which other beings move.

At the most basic level, our embodiment makes possible the awareness of other bodies. I see other bodies; the haptic sense of being touched and of touching, established in infancy, informs me that I will encounter another body if I continue to walk toward that other body. As simple as this may sound, it is the source of an insight with far-reaching implications: **embodiment grounds the inevitability of sociality**.

Human embodiment is not, as we have seen, merely an inert unconscious vehicle in which the true self lives. Thus, two embodied selves encountering each other are unlike two automobiles colliding. Embodiment is always "imaged." It is self-conscious, a source of identity and memory. The self-consciousness inherent in human spatiality carries with it an awareness that there are other selves, selves who are not-my-self. Since it alerts the self to the **there** (where the other self is) as well as to the **here** (where the self is), this awareness engenders a sense of separation as well as of unity. Our awareness of the other brings to light the unavoidable fact of **relation**, the fact that we are in some way related to others. This fact points to the normative question of **how we should relate**.

It is spatiality which makes us aware of self and of otherness, thus promoting our consciousness of relation. Indeed, spatiality itself facilitates relation; it is, after all, always but not exclusively through our embodiment that we relate. We are thereby enabled to see and to hear, to touch and to smell the other. Moreover, through our own experience of embodiment and social spatiality we are able to understand **something** of the other.

Our entire lives are so interrelated with others that we

could not exist outside of physical relationship. That is clearly the case with infants, but throughout our lives we are shaped by others and we shape others. We enable them into being who they are, and they us. As a matter of fact we could not even be individuals without others.[19]

The physical basis of our social relations establishes them as natural. That has important implications. A second argument has the effect of deflating human pretensions or, better, elevating our appreciation of natural life. That concerns the sociality of another species, hogs.

What is the culture of pigs? Wherein lies their piggishness? Let us consider wild pigs. Feral swine generally have aggressive dispositions and live in herds of four to twenty foraging animals including one to four females and their young. Wild boars range freely in forest settings throughout the year, staying close to the herd in reproduction season, at which time they become territorial and protective. Omnivorous and voracious eaters, sows and boars alike spend the majority of their waking hours walking, rooting, and eating.

The courtship of an oestrus female by a wild boar lasts several days, with the male grunting a soft rhythmic mating song and having to overcome a last minute rebuttal from the female who typically wheels and faces him just before he tries to mount her. The wild sow often spends days making a nest for her young. The boar seems to enjoy the presence of piglets, tolerating them as they wiggle on top of him when he rests.[20]

Clearly there is a sociality of wild pig culture, and it is natural. Our own sociality is natural as well. It is natural in a distinctive way, just as is the life-cycle of the boar's affection for piglets/subsequent departure from the family/annual return to mate. I am not equating the two. We will examine one aspect of our human species' distinctive natural capacities and culture shortly.

Spirituality

Joining embodiment and sociality as part of our natural, spatial constitution is symbolization. That is the ability of humankind and other conscious animals (and possibly plants) to signify. Here we will concentrate on human spirituality. My claim here is that spirituality itself is natural.

Human beings are driven to discover meaning in the bio-social conditions that they both inhabit and establish.[21] This drive is not an intellectual puzzle or an intentional project, such as working out a mathematical problem or balancing a checkbook. We don't have to decide to do it. Rather there is something within us that pushes us to make sense of the varied experiences we have. We want to connect, to integrate them. John Dewey described the "feel" of this process when he wrote, "Reflection is natural and continuous."[22] The most graphic example of the drive to meaning is when we face the death of a parent, grandparent, or child. Another is when we become aware of a social injustice or personal betrayal. Yet another is suddenly viewing a landscape of sweeping beauty.

One of the things these examples have in common is that they are all relational.[23] They all raise questions about our individual lives. We feel them personally, and at the same time they are evoked by relationships with other people or other natural entities. Our lives are not atomistically self-contained or mechanical. As a matter of fact, we consider those who live self-contained lives abnormal in some way—autistic, psychotic, reclusive, sociopathic, etc. We cannot escape our embodiment or sociality, both of which are relationally constituted. Relationship is even more at the heart of the drive for meaning and thus, of spirituality.

As we have been discussing it, spirituality is not some set

of beliefs that we give assent to. It is a feeling, a holistic experience that is first visceral and only then reflective/cognitive. Particularly today people are hungry for a sense of meaning that transcends scientific explanation or psychological dynamics. We long to find a spirituality that relieves the emptiness we experience.[24] What we are hungry for cannot be forced. We cannot think our way into it; we cannot buy it. Rather the best we can do is to be open to discovering it. **To be authentic the spirituality we seek must be one that we feel in our bones**. It must arise from deep inside or sweep over us from outside, or both. We cannot manufacture it; we must feel it as being beyond our conscious control. If it is not, then it will not satisfy. William Yeats encapsulates this insight in saying, "We only believe those thoughts which have been conceived not in the brain but in the whole body."[25]

We got a glimpse of this spirituality in chapter 3 when we identified one source of religious zeal for the environment as the feelings of connectedness and transcendence. Later we affirmed the Christian belief that this sense of connectedness and transcendence comes from the fact that the earth is God's home. We have suggested the metaphor that the earth is God's home created for all living entities, and thus home for the human and all other species. If those affirmations are true, then we would expect to find God present in nature. The assertion that spirituality is natural should come as no surprise. Rather it can be seen as axiomatic. God is present in an essential and all-pervading way.

Indeed, this is relatively old-hat theologically. What else was St. Augustine saying when he wrote, "Our hearts are restless until they find their rest in thee?"[26] Indeed, even John Calvin could say that "God is nature, if one said that with proper qualifications and reverential attitude."[27] The same point was being made by Pope John Paul II when he said that if humanity is not at peace with God, "then earth itself cannot be at peace."[28]

In line with these views, Jay McDaniel offers what has proved to be a personally helpful spiritual insight. He speaks of the "lure of God" as operating within us and also outside of us.[29] What I find particularly attractive is that this begins to specify **how** God is present in us and outside us. It does so without sacrificing human autonomy. Thus it is entirely compatible with our assertion that spirituality is natural. In the sense that God enfolds the entire world and feels with and for it, we all experience the lure of God.

This also means that there is an objective reality "out there" **and** "in here." God exists. God exists in nature as well as in history. The fact that we have held humankind to be primarily historical has rendered God a matter of choice. If a group felt God to be present in its history, that was all well and good. If a group didn't, then that was fine, too. This at least appeared to make God only a matter of confession or interpretation. The group's interpretation of its history, when elevated to the dominant criterion of existence, made God appear rather subjective—a matter of personal preference. When one asks, "Which history?" then God may or may not be present. When one asks, "Whose ozone layer? Whose nature? Whose space?," then the choice is to include or exclude the objective reality of God. It is no longer possible to subjectivize that choice and render God trivial by dint of being a matter of human preference.[30]

The Place of Human Distinctiveness

The framework of spatiality which we have outlined assists us in viewing God as Lord of history and nature. Rather than reducing God to nature it indicates that the presence of God in natural processes establishes God's sovereignty. That sovereignty is not a matter of autocratic rule but compassionate presence. God does not override nature but is actively present in nature.

It is from within this theological framework that we can inquire as to the distinctive place of the human species within nature, within God's world. Some people might have interpreted my claim that human beings are natural as a depreciation of who we are as a species. That is not my intention. Rather it is to see our naturalness as an enabling limitation, a grounding of possibilities in reality. It begins to suggest a way of being in the world that connects us with others. This anthropology reduces the likelihood that we will see ourselves as machines or see nature as inert material. We will not so easily objectify the physical world or reduce nature to things. Rather, it encourages the view that human beings exist in dynamic relation with the remainder of living beings.

We have claimed that human life, while it is natural, has a distinctive place in nature. Exactly what that place is becomes a matter of great import. The difficulties that this discussion typically produces arise from its being motivated by a desire to establish the superiority of the human. Differentiating people from other animals has often taken place in the context of making a dichotomous comparison to justify human control over nature.

In the present context the claim of human distinctiveness is not intended to establish superiority or reject kinship. All species have a unique place in the biosphere. We are a significant species but we are not the sole focus of God's care; we are not superior beings who own the world as home.

Human life is natural. The symbiosis of our own with the roles of others presses us to understand human activity in concert with the whole. The primary dynamic, we can now understand, is not competition but synergy. The view of earth we are presenting expands the conception of synergy to include not only the traditional components of plants, mineral life, soil, animals, and humankind, but also God.

So, we are now ready to consider the distinctive role of the species in relation to the earth. That includes our relation to each other, whose fuller dimensions we will take up in chapter 6. It also includes our relation to God. Here we will be content to inquire primarily as to the particular role of the human vis-à-vis the rest of the natural world.[31] One way of boldly formulating this question is to ask, "What are people for?" **One answer to this question centers around the capacity of human beings for responsibility.**

Other historical answers to this question have been many. The discussion here has not been so much concerned to maintain distinctiveness as it has been oriented to the discovery of right relationships. Right relationships will further the creator's desire for the flourishing of all life. The place of the human is to relate to all life as God would have us relate to it. We have been endowed by God and are continually lured by God to responsible living.

In what does this human responsibility consist? One persuasive argument locates human distinctiveness in its self-conscious moral dimension. Human beings are those thinking, symbolizing creatures who can imagine the consequences of their action. They can compare one way of acting with another and can decide to act in one way or another.

It may have been otherwise in the past but at present the activities of the human species seem to be those most influential in shaping the future of the planet. One can imagine that dinosaurs were such a species in the past. We began this volume by looking at phyloplankton; their continued well-being may be crucial to ongoing ecological health. You have noticed, however, that in the case of both dinosaurs and phyloplankton they are more acted upon than acting. Humans are both.

Other candidates for "most influential" are the great apes and other "higher order" mammals. What distinguishes humankind from them is the greater range of considerations that enter into human decision-making. In short, human beings can be held accountable for much of what happens to other species and for a longer time frame than can any other mammals. Accountability is, of course, directly correlated with responsibility.

Not so parenthetically, it is important to note that the responsibility of human beings is limited because human capacity is limited. People can only be responsible for what lies within their capacity. Frequently we flagellate ourselves or wallow in guilt for what lies beyond our reach. More often we let an unlimited sense of responsibility deter us from exercising the capacity we do have.

A second distinctive feature of humankind is the stimulus to worship. Other species may sense an uplifting drive to praise God and a lure to live in response to God's graciousness. They may feel awe when they encounter the goodness of God's home. They **may**, but at present we **know** that humanity responds in this way.

The distinctiveness of humankind has been connected with the **imago dei**. This "image of God" is that which Genesis 1:26 describes as God's intention, "Let us create **ahdam** (literally, earth creature) in our own image." This has often been used simply to baptize human superiority. Jay McDaniel makes another, intriguing suggestion. He identifies the **imago dei** as the capacity to care:

> . . . the possibilities of **imago dei** are for an inwardly felt affection—a care—that can enrich our intelligence and imagination, and that can inform our ac-

tion. To be made in the image of God is to have within ourselves possibilities for care that approximate the divine care.[32]

The reason that McDaniel's suggestion is so attractive to me is because it combines the two distinctively human capacities we have noted: responsibility and worship. Worship is the outward activity that corresponds to "an inwardly felt affection." Responsibility motivated by a worshipful attitude transcends compulsory obligation and becomes "care that approximates the divine care."

Toward Caring Action

We are now ready to turn our attention toward the moral implications of our being constituted as home places for other natural beings and for each other. What does this understanding of our being natural imply? What does it mean to relate to plants, animals, and people as though they were God's home?

Clearly the way we have described human beings' distinctive place in the world has a great deal to do with answering those questions. Beings who are responsible and worshipful should live out who they are. Being caring creatures is both who we are and what we should do.

The next chapter begins to explore how to live out our relationships—first with other species and then with each other.

6

Homemaking

Sometimes when we are faced with a quandary we ask others for advice. "What should I do?" we ask. Many times the other person says, "Just be yourself." This advice is both reassuring and frustrating. It is essentially the moral advice we offered at the end of chapter 5.

It is reassuring to know that our decisions and style of living grow out of ourselves. It is also frustrating because we know that we are many things. It is not so easy to know which of our selves we should be.

We may act in ways that build up our environment **and** in ways that diminish its quality. That is what this chapter is about. How, on the basis of who we are, can we make this earth a good home? How can we be good stewards of ourselves, others and all life? At the end of chapter 5 we had reached the conclusion that being ourselves meant being caring, responsible, and worshipful beings. Just what all does that mean? That is our question.

The ethic of homemaking flows out of the theological perspective we have developed. The basic principle of the ethic is to "be yourself" in relation to God, to self, to other species, and to other people. It is those relationships that will organize our discussion.

Relating to God

One distinctive quality of humankind is that we are worshipping beings. We sense a divine lure beyond ourselves; we are engaged in an ongoing search for meaning and purpose. God has created us to be her children, her family. Thus it is entirely natural that we worship God.

When we think of worshipping God, we typically picture a formal worship service. That is unfortunate. If God is present in the world continually luring us to himself, then we are **continually** in God's world living in some relation to God. We are, in effect, worshipping or not worshipping God throughout our lives. Our relationship to God permeates our lives and our relationships—to our selves, to other species, and to other people.

One aspect of worshipping God involves spirituality, the living out of our devotion to God in "religious" ways. Another aspect, only artificially conceived of as separate from spirituality, is morality. We worship through living the Christian life. It is on morality that we are focusing in this chapter.

The other two distinctive aspects of ourselves—being caring and being responsible beings—have to do with morality. The Christian tradition has plainly stated that we respond to God's goodness by living caring, responsible lives. Thus we worship God by relating to creation in the ways in which God created us to do so. In effect, the morality of our other relationships grows out of, and is one way of, worshipping God.

Relating to Our Selves

Often this relationship is neglected in contemporary ethics. Those who emphasize virtue and the character of the self do take some note of it. Those who stress decision-making often ignore it altogether.

The framework articulated thus far in this book leads to several distinctive emphases, not the least of which is the relation of the self to itself. If we are home and are part of God's home, then ethics is not external to us. It is not just a matter of caring for others, but also of caring for our own selves. So our own self-interests as those who live in symbiosis with others and God cannot be separated from our relationships. It's not a matter of us versus them. Taking this seriously means that ethics involves living in ways that respect and realize our most worshipful possibilities. It is in our own self-interest to respect and care for others. This is not to condone the pursuit of selfish interests while pretending that we live in relation. To pursue self-interest in opposition to others is not to be who we were designed to be. That is not to be who we, in fact, are. To live in competition or antagonism with God's other creatures **is to live in opposition to our selves.**

We have the capacity to do that. We can live in unworshipful ways. That is self-destructive, however—it is not to care for ourselves, not to be responsible to ourselves. We call people who do not care for themselves pathological. They are **self**-destructive because they cannot care for **others** unless they care for themselves. To be a healthy human being we must live in relationship. To pursue our self-interest is to pursue the interests of others. There is an African saying from Zimbabwe that summarizes this reality. When one person asks another, "How are you today?" the person answers, "I am well if you are well." What we are suggesting is that God designed the world to be, in essence, synergistic. My health depends on your health and the health of other species and biospheric members. Conversely, yours depends on mine and on that of other natural beings.

So then, if the world is home, to worship God is to love oneself as a member of the whole. From this emerges an attitude, a moral disposition, to care for oneself in cooperative connection. **What that means is quite complicated.** I would not have that complexity disguised by our apparently simple moral framework. For example, we know that to love oneself

as a member of the whole involves (1) a responsibility and
respect toward oneself (2) in relation to others. So there are
two poles: responsibility to self and to others. The two **are not**
essentially dichotomous as some contemporary ethics picture them.

What sort of guideposts might we offer to express our
moral relation to ourselves? What does homemaking mean in
relation to ourselves?

1. Enjoying our selves. This guidepost suggests that part
of glorifying God is to enjoy our created selves. It means that
we appreciate and live in harmony with who we are. Often we
take enjoying ourselves to mean having a good time. That is
true in a more profound way than we usually think it.

Reflect on the times when you have enjoyed yourself.
Usually they happen when you act in ways that respect your
own gifts, the gifts of others, and the physical joys of the world.
You act in ways that are appropriate to the best in you, that
recognize the place of others, and often appreciate the material world around you. There is a sense of relaxation even in
the midst of challenge.

Integral to this, I believe, is the ability to accept our own
limitations and the limitations of the situation. Living in essential agreement with our nature means both not underesti-
mating our being nor overestimating it. Often our failure to
enjoy derives either from overloading ourselves or from being
lethargic.

Similarly, enjoying cannot be equated either with consuming, as it often is, or not consuming, as some ascetic philosophies maintain. Rather, enjoying involves consuming those
things that are healthy for us in appropriate amounts. Too
often consumption has been used as a substitute for community,[1] or as a surrogate for self-esteem.

2. Healing broken relations. It may seem strange to include this guidepost in a section on relating to oneself. Never-

theless, actively pursuing wellness and right relations is part of the respect we owe ourselves. We need to ask others' forgiveness, and vice versa. Healing is part of being compassionate, of feeling-with others and the world. To participate in restoring broken relations is part of the sense of justice that dwells within us, that God lures us toward.

It may be, of course, that we cannot heal brokenness; that may be one of our limitations. We may only be able to stand with others in their disease. We may only be able to retard the pollution of the planet or only moderately aid in regenerating the earth. Nevertheless, acting on a sense of justice and compassion is an important way we relate to our selves. It is one way we respect our selves.

3. Respecting dignity. A venerable part of Catholic moral theology emphasizes human rights on the basis of the God-given dignity of human beings.[2] That dignity extends to the rest of the biota and to our selves.

In its simplest terms it calls us to recognize the value of our selves. We all have the right to participate in enjoying the world and to be taken seriously. This issues in political and civil activity when there is a threat to dignity. We participate not for ourselves alone but as representatives of other living beings.

Respecting our dignity also implies a responsibility to educate ourselves in the moral life. We are responsible for the moral formation of our own character. So we participate in those activities and institutions that will school us in virtue. We can be intentional in choosing those activities that will dispose us to be upstanding Christian family members, citizens, and workers.

4. Caring for our bodies. Relating to our selves rightly and enjoying ourselves includes taking care of our bodies. Avoiding those substances that destroy our capacity to contribute to our common life is only one part of this. Exercising, stimulating our mental health, and avoiding obsessive over-work are also aspects of right relations. Cultivating our bodily well-being is integral to the other guideposts mentioned here.

One of the best examples of how our own lives are in-terrelated with other peoples' and the earth's comes from this area. Those who study nutrition are finding that the most ecologically responsible agriculture produces the foods that are most healthful for us. Eating lower on the food chain puts less pressure on the land and less pressure on our hearts. Sus-tainable agriculture actually regenerates the land and offers promise for future generations to enjoy their lives.

Thus, homemaking begins close to home, by promoting our own well-being.

Relating to Other Species

A recent incident during the Iowa Pork Congress illus-trates the way we too often pit care for the environment over against care for human beings. A member of PETA, People for the Equal Treatment of Animals, threw a pie in the face of the Pork Queen.

Later there was a series of ads timed to coincide with the Iowa State Farm. One ad in the *Des Moines Register* (August 9, 1991) protested the way livestock were being raised in Iowa. It compared the slaughter of animals with the grisly Dahmer murders in Milwaukee. A second projected ad headlined "Meat Stinks!" was refused.

This sort of inflammatory behavior only reinforces the dichotomy between people and animals on both the "human-ists' " and the environmentalists' part. **Both** groups regard care for other species and care for humankind as opposing values!

The morality of homemaking, based on being ourselves,

issues in an opposite principle: **People should respect animal, plant, and nonsentient life because our flourishing depends on their flourishing.** Thus we must look beyond a mentality where, for example, only people **or** only animals win, to one where both species can thrive.

The very way our society frames environmental questions often precludes creative moral thinking.[3] Indeed, the very way questions are framed or described carries moral values. A Christian communitarian ethic is built precisely on relationality which asserts that the health and well-being of the whole is primary to that of its parts.[4] Such a framework precludes an atomistic or adversarial basepoint.

A second principle that we have been employing is that our moral dispositions and behavior should be appropriate to our relationships. Though we share kinship features with animals and to a lesser extent plants, we humans have distinctive capacities and responsibilities. What is the nature of our relationship? How does that guide our moral attitudes and actions?

Our relation to other species, we have seen, is one of interdependent kinship. We are responsible for caring for God's creatures because they are valuable in themselves, to God, and to us. They constitute our home and we theirs. The nature of our relationship, therefore, calls us to two tasks. It calls us to respect other species as having intrinsic value, just as we have value beyond what we can do or be for others. Second, it calls us to act in ways that sustain the goodness of created life for the biosphere. Our relationship thus calls us to respect life in itself and to take care for the future generativity of the planet.

Within this frame, we are often confronted by particular issues. Each situation presents some different features. We do not have the same relationship with the rain forests, the peoples of eastern Germany, the snail darter, and the phytoplankton. Therefore, we cannot hope to give moral answers to every environmental question here. **Each ecological situation calls for our best moral deliberation since each species has its own integrity.**

Nevertheless we can establish a theological and moral framework. That is precisely what we have been doing. We can even enunciate moral guidelines on the basis of that framework. Each species has its own integrity, but it also shares features with the rest of us **and** it also exists in relation to the whole.

Operating within a framework of respect and care, what guidelines can we offer? If caring for other species is a way of caring for oneself, then the four guidelines we described earlier could be used to spell out what respect and care for other species mean. The World Council of Churches suggests three principles for the "good society"—justice, participation, and sustainability.[5] We will check our four against their three as a way of insuring that we are in line with the world church's thinking.

1. Enjoying other species. This may seem a strange guideline to some. We expect moral rules to state an obligation, but seldom encourage a pleasure. And what does that mean? Maybe we don't think morality can be pleasurable. Maybe it is an instance of the separation of body and mind, that we are suspicious of what feels good.

It is a guideline I would commend, because taking the time to enjoy the world of nature, to enjoy our home, has significant moral ramifications. One of those is simply that we will take better care of animals and plants and land if we enjoy them. An old Jewish proverb states that we will have to answer to God not only for those sins we commit but also for all the pleasures we fail to enjoy. Amen! God save us from an anti-leisure, anti-materialist theology and ethics. I cannot imagine a worse prescription for the environment. Or for ourselves.

God designed the world as a good home for all species. Thus it is right that all participate and enjoy their home to the greatest possible extent. This participation and enjoyment extends to all species and to the future generations of all species. What this means for humankind is that we have the responsibility to enjoy and to sustain the conditions that allow ourselves and others to enjoy the world.

2. Healing broken relations. In some instances it is not sufficient to sustain existing conditions. We need to regenerate the health of ecosystems that are endangered. A World Council document states: "God's work of redemption in Jesus Christ reconciles all things and calls us to the healing work of the Spirit in all creation."[6]

For some species, it is simply too late. The best we can do is to cease endangering other species—through alleviating acid rainfall, lowering the rate of ozone depletion, protecting those threatened by extinction. This is an issue of justice, justice defined as the regard or respect that a being deserves. Too often justice has been defined in us-versus-them terms. From our perspective, practicing justice in our relations with other species is a matter of paying respect in our actions. It implies the restitution of right relations, healing, and the maintenance of healthy systems. That healing does not diminish us; rather, it builds our self-respect.

3. Respecting dignity. Healing broken relations between ourselves and other species is based on the dignity of all species. The justice guideline we have been describing expresses that respect. If we ask why all species have dignity, why they have value, then we Christians would give a theological answer. God gave value to all her creatures; they remain valuable to God. Notice that we are not claiming that all species and all individuals have an absolute right to be preserved. However, respecting dignity means that we should act in ways that allow creatures to be who they are. We should not mistreat animals, plants, or people.

This guideline has to do with justice but also with participation. The dignity inherent in humankind points to their having a voice in decisions that affect them. This is the moral bedrock of democratic government. What does that imply for the voiceless—animals, rocks, and plants—that cannot speak for themselves? Gary Comstock suggests that these species have an interest, if not a voice, in their future.[7] That has the moral impact of increasing human accountability. It is our privilege and responsibility to promote the interests of all beings toward making this planet really our home.

The dignity due all species is also a matter of wisdom having been encoded into them. Humankind may do well to listen to the wisdom of nature. We can learn from other species and can relate to them, even if we cannot understand their voices.

4. Caring for others' bodies. What does this guideline imply for our relations with other species? A literal care for other individual bodies suggests doing those things that sustain life. That includes all species-life. Here the norm of sustainability comes into view. Continuing to consume petroleum at present rates is not sustainable. Continuing to do so is not to care for our bodies. It is no more to care for them than to continue to eat foods high in fat, cholesterol, and calories.

This brings into view a more figurative use of "bodies." What about the whole ecological body of the future? How can we care for others' and our present bodies in ways that promote a healthy environment for future badgers, foxes, and rhododendrons? The norm of acting in regenerative, sustainable ways presses itself upon us more and more.

Perhaps it is distortive even to speak of the use of "body" as figurative. That is to discount our body's connection with the bodies of animals and plants and the biotic pyramid. Merleau-Ponty's work points to our living bodies as one cell within the living, sentient, indeed self-sensing, body of the world. It is Merleau-Ponty's genius to affirm that: "For the first time in modern philosophy, human beings with all of their language and thoughts are enveloped within the atmosphere of this planet, an atmosphere which circulates both inside and outside of their bodies."[8] The biosphere is itself alive. Finding ourselves in the world involves understanding the presence of animals who are our link to the **flesh** of the world.[9] Right relations with other species are ultimately right relations with ourselves.

Relating to Other People

Pope John Paul II asserts that: "Not only has God given the earth to man, who must use it with respect for the original good purpose . . . but man too is God's gift to man. He must therefore respect the natural and moral structure."[10] John Paul reveals a wholistic understanding of the environment when he speaks of these natural and moral structures as a "social ecology."[11]

If, as we claimed, the environment includes not only ourself but also other species, then surely a theology and ethics of the environment cannot exclude our relating with others of our own species. Seldom does an environmental theology deal with other people, though, they are a highly significant part of the earth.

On the other hand, the discipline of ethics deals almost exclusively with interpersonal and social issues. Often ethics includes consideration of ecology as one issue among others. I am reversing this order. Environmental ethics is the overarching category; human-human relationships are one aspect of this theology and ethics.

Since the discipline of ethics has been preoccupied with human relations, much insightful thinking has taken place. What might we add of a distinctive stripe from our environmental perspective? Our framework has stressed several features: one is a stronger grounding of the **corporate** nature of the species; a second is the way nonhuman nature makes human life both possible and enjoyable; a third is the corporeal, material, spatial aspects of the self and the world; a fourth is the claim that relationships are the heart of the self.

What is perhaps most distinctive here is that the ethics which emerges is more oriented toward enhancing the quality of our home life than it is a matter of calculating what our obligations are. It is less focused on the minimum necessary for civil life, or what one ought to do, or even what we **owe** each other and other species. It is more focused on offering a vision of what our home might be, were we to live up to who we are.

We have claimed that each of us is **internally related** to the life of the world. McDaniel describes what this means: "One living being is 'internally related' to others if the organism's relations to those others are partly constitutive of the organism's own essence."[12] The case that we are internally related to phytoplankton or drinking water can be legitimately made. However, that we are internally related to other people is quite evident. The quality of our life depends upon our interaction with God, self, nature, and other humans. We exist in a web of relations in which physical, psychic, social, and spiritual characteristics interpenetrate.

What guidelines can we suggest about relating to our own species? We offer here an exploration of the four benchmarks we used in the previous sections on relating to our selves and to other species. The implicit claim is that, if we are internally related to self and to other species as well as to other people, these guidelines can be illuminative here as well. Rather than presenting full expositions of these guidelines, we will be content to suggest implications distinctive to our framework.

1. Enjoying other human beings. Again, an injunction to pleasure seems strangely out of place here. The more I think about it, however, the more profound the experience of enjoyment appears. To be able to enjoy other people requires a certain relaxation, a somewhat secure self-esteem, and perhaps also a freedom from threat. Much of what we enjoy about life we enjoy as a direct result of our relations with others of our species. To be open to others, then, is to be able to enjoy them. So enjoyment is a rather significant experience. Our capacity to be open and to enjoy others promotes a sense of real well-being, of being at home.

This raises the question: "What conditions are required to be able to enjoy others?" The answer to that question is surprising: **Enjoying other people requires a rough equality with them.** Most simply, we cannot enjoy those who threaten us or those we feel pity for. The situation of inequality is reflected in toxic dumps being located in proximity to minority groups' neighborhoods. That inequality derives from and reinforces the failure to enjoy others of different racial and ethnic groups.

The more basic situation is that of equality, however. This can be measured in terms of equal value in God's eyes, similarity of physical constitution, or roughly similar years of life span. Our limitations and our futures are more equal than unequal, especially if we look at them through corporate, physical, and relational lenses. Those with greater power and affluence may escape the impact of toxic conditions longer, but they may enjoy life very little more than the less affluent and powerful. They may enjoy life less. My point is that enjoying other people—learning from them, sharing affection—points to the need for rough equality with others. That equality can be specified as the minimum of resources needed to free people from the threat of others and to lead them to develop a sense of self-esteem.

2. Healing broken relations. The work of forgiveness and reconciliation is vast. Indeed, healing broken relations with other people is at least as enormous a task as healing relations with other species. One relation calling for healing is the rift between the industrialized North and the developing South. The issue of global warming cries for united action. "Leaders struggling with the hand-to-mouth survival of millions find that 'sacrifice today to save tomorrow' is bitter medicine, especially when those administering it have already reaped the benefits of unlimited greenhouse effusions. Attributing global warming to developing countries like India and China is an 'excellent example of environmental colonialism'. . . ."[13]

This very urgent situation does admit a way of beginning to heal relations. The expanding energy demands of the South will exacerbate carbon emissions. However, "with financial support from industrial countries, motivated in part by their desire to avert an atmospheric calamity, and Third World commitments to improve energy efficiency, North and South could strike the global bargain that is begging to be made."[14]

Let us turn from this planetary example of healing relations to more ordinary ones. A routine everyday habit of maintaining good relations with others or healing broken relations would develop a pattern of care. A pattern of care for others is unimaginable apart from a pattern of care for self and for other species. Indeed, genuine caring for the self inevitably involves care for the other, and vice versa.[15] Caring for self, other species, and other human beings develop simultaneously. Indeed, I suspect that carelessness for self, for others, and for the environment are linked as well.

3. Respecting dignity. This guideline suggests that the whole of the moral life is not social. The individual maintains individual consciousness, body, and value which calls us to respect what stands over against us. If the guideline of enjoyment suggested the norm of equality, this one hints at freedom. We are to respect the dignity of the other, her freedom, her right even not to participate. Indeed we have to protect freedom from coercion if our relationships, especially with other people, are to be meaningful.

The specter of conflict comes into view here. If we are to respect the dignity of all people and other species, what happens when one's dignity is opposed to the interest of others? Is one's dignity more essential than the interest of others? How are dignity and interests to be differentiated? Adjudicated? These questions arise from assumptions about individual rights and interests. Perhaps what is needed is a redefinition of dignity as being **corporate** but which also maintains the value of the individual.

Our dignity as individuals inheres finally in our participation in the common good.[16] That common good must include the ecosphere. As Christians we maintain that everyone is a child of God with their own autonomous value and, hence, dignity. The common good cannot override the individual without ceasing to be genuinely the common good.

This guideline implies the necessity of rearranging the system of distribution so that the common good of all is served without violating the dignity of any. That is a tall order. One way of beginning that rearrangement would be to inaugurate procedures of decision-making that were more broadly participatory. We will be able to test this most challenging conundrum in our next chapter, on the economics of the environment.

4. Caring for other people's bodies. At a minimum this guideline points to a concern for other people's health and well-being. Caring for others' bodies involves wanting them to have a standard of living that meets their physical needs in a way that can be sustained into the future. The care that we pay to our own physical welfare becomes a measure of our care for others. Clearly this is what Christ meant in counselling his disciples to love neighbors as they loved themselves.

This goes far beyond the principle of nonmalfeasance, the injunction not to harm others. That principle is based on a view of our life together that is atomistic. It suggests that all we owe others is not to hurt them. This signals a view of human nature that emphasizes the separation of individuals from others. That view is incorporated into libertarian and capitalist philosophies and has had incredible impact in the United States and other western countries. It leads to ecological disaster. This book is based on diametrically opposing axioms.

The norm of caring for others' bodies extends beyond seeing that others' physical needs are met. Caring for bodies involves meeting the spiritual and social needs of others as well—for demonstrations of affection, for the willingness to share bread and wine, for being present with others. As we are together with others we find our own needs met as well. The word "need" connotes a paternalistic, condescending attitude until we realize that we all need each other. We need each other if our lives are going to be complete and if we are going to enjoy our selves and others. The theological assumption **here** is that we cannot be complete without other people and other species. God designed the world to be a community of interactive relationships. **That is what home is.**

At this point we have said a bit about what it means to be

human, to be worshipful, to be caring, to be responsible. We have looked at four basic, defining relationships: to God, to self, to other species, and to other people. We have even begun to fill in some moral guidelines.

This discussion may not have become specific enough for you. "What can I do?" you may ask. There is an explosion of good books which answer that question.[17] One of my favorites is the 365 Ways to Save the Environment Calendar. However, what is important here is for you to decide how, specifically, you can care for the environment and yourself. God wants you and me to enjoy our lives and to enable others, of all species, to do likewise.

The next chapter will become more specific. By using the perspective developed in the first six chapters, it will approach the most difficult environmental issue, how to reconcile economics and ecology. This will provide a test of our theory as well as more specific guides to action.

Home Finances

What remains is perhaps the most difficult task of all. It is difficult because its scope is broad. It is difficult because Christian theologians have not ventured into this terrain often. It is difficult because it puts aesthetically pleasing theory to the test. It is also the single most significant factor in ecological renewal.

The future of the environment is an economic issue. Consider the questions that are contained there:

How are humankind and the earth related?

What provisions will be made to insure the future quality of nature, and hence ourselves?

What structures of accountability can and should be established to insure sustainable distribution?

There is an economic dimension to all environmental questions. If we slight these questions of who pays, and who benefits, then we are really playing games. We are not serious about renewing the health of the ecosphere.

It frankly alarms me that so few environmentalists address the economic issue in their writing.[1] This is troublesome in books written from a philosophical perspective and even more so if the perspective is Christian. This is hardly accidental. Rather, both economics and Christian theology in Euro-

America have insulated themselves from environmental issues. How that has happened is important to its amelioration.

In this chapter we are claiming nothing less than this:

Our economy is strangling us.

It is strangling our environment, our bodies, our community.

This will continue so long as we ignore the interrelation of our economy and the environment.

This chapter begins by looking at the reasons behind the insulation of economics from ecology, from our bodies, and from a concern for community. It then suggests an expanded notion of economics which includes the whole of nature, including the human species. After formulating a Christian theological perspective on the economics of God as the next step, the chapter concludes with a set of moral guidelines on our economy.

The Separation of Economics

One reason why our economy is strangling us comes from the way we view economics. Essentially, we see the economy as an infinitely complex machine which operates independently of us. Structural as well as attitudinal elements lie behind the disconnection we perceive between economics and our lives. Our system of economics fosters this view, and Christian theology has acquiesced in this separation. Thus, in what follows, I will examine ways in which both the economic system and Christian thought have contributed to the separation and strangulation.

1. The strangulation of nature. Aldo Leopold suggested that not until we begin to see nature "as a community to which we belong" will we begin to "use it with love and respect." Instead, "we abuse the land because we see it as a commodity belonging to us."[2] While Leopolds's statement is powerful, we need to move beyond it and ask **why** that is true.

We have made the case in this book that the basic problem, as Leopold notes, is the disconnection we feel with our home, the natural world. Economics has contributed to this in two ways. First, our economic system has externalized the impact of our method of distributing goods and services (economics) from nature. Second, economics has obscured nature from its considerations by reducing it to a commodity or property relation. Let me explain.

Externalization. First, our system of economics has ignored the impact it has on the environment. For example, the price of a bushel of corn excludes the value of the topsoil eroded by its growth.[3] The refining of crude oil into gasoline excludes the air and thermal pollution involved in its manufacture. The costs of metals and minerals do not reflect the long-term effects of their extraction on the environment.

The underlying dynamic is that air, water, topsoil, wild animals, and plants are in the public domain. If no one has to pay for these goods, then the costs to the environment and, of course, to us are excluded—externalized—from view. If no one has to pay for them, then we can conveniently forget them. At least for the present, the real costs of production do not get included in the price of the products we consume. A system of economics which only takes account of production and consumption in monetary terms ignores the long-term impact on the environment. As Wendell Berry writes, "The singular demand for production has been unable to acknowledge the importance of the sources of production in nature and in human culture."[4] The real cost of food and of other goods has been narrowed to the price we pay at the cash register.

We are viewing the costs to nature of translating what belongs to all of us into private commodities. The enjoyment of nature has become a matter of what the private individual can afford. Nature is something we enjoy at the Grand Canyon or Florida beaches, if we can afford to vacation there.

Reduction to Property. Second, our economy has excluded nature from consideration by reducing it to a property relation. This is the result of economics' claim to be autonomous, to operate only according to its own internal dynamics. Bruce Douglass asserts that from the time when the foundations of our modern economic system were laid, "it has been part and parcel of the modern experience unto itself, governed by its own logic and pursuing its own discrete ends."[5] Nature got swallowed up into economics laws.

Understanding how this happened is vital to our seeing that economics has strangled nature, and also our bodies and community. John Cobb and Herman Daly, in their book, *For the Common Good*, charge that land and nature have been reduced to "property relations." Nature has become merely a cost to be factored in. Before that happened, " the wild facts would be self-evidently important to economics. But when land has become a property relation" [as, for example, rent, or mortgage payments], "distinct from other property relations in rather minor respects, then it is much more one commodity among others than a factor of production. The forces of nature, indeed nature in general, have disappeared from view. Economics as a discipline floats free from the physical world."[6]

For example, if land is thought of economically at all, then it is thought of as a price commodity, traded on the Chicago Board of Trade. Note, as well, the total lack of a **communal relation** to land. Economics is thus structurally insensitive to its impact on the environment and to the effects of environmental deterioration on the economy.

For economic theory value is to be found solely in the **satisfaction of human desires**. We can see this gradual loss of interest in the physical world, in the shift of attention from:

land, labor, and capital TO
landlords, laborers, and capitalists TO
rents, wages, and profits.

The economic terms become more abstract as we go along. Features of this world that cannot be assigned a monetary price disappear from economic science. Please note that human beings were not assumed to be part of the physical world. We have lost touch with ourselves.

Briefly, let us consider some of the consequences when economics forgets land:

1. Economics makes us forget that resources are finite, limited. One economist at a World Bank conference, for example, said that: "The notion that there are limits that can't be taken care of by capital has to be rejected."[7]

2. Economists think that capital can always be substituted for land. This breaks down, of course, in the face of massive environmental crisis. But when land is reduced to a commodity then we fall into the notion of substitutability. When our groundwater is contaminated, however, there is simply no substitute. You can't drink money.

3. **We forget** that we are interconnected to a biospheric community. More and more the fate of the natural world becomes concentrated in the hands of those conglomerates whose economists are structurally blinded from including nature in their projections. We who support and benefit from this economic system are hardly free from blame.

Christian Acquiescence. We have explored in chapter 2

some of the factors that led to Christianity's insensitivity to the environment. Those feed into the relative neglect of economics in Christian thought, a neglect made particularly urgent by the significance of economics. Fortunately, considerable attention has been recently paid to the human impact of economic systems, and particularly to the questions of poverty and the redistribution of income. Especially commendable in this regard is the Bishops' Pastoral on the Economy.[8] Unfortunately, much less attention has been paid to the connection between economics and the environment.

The schism that separates humankind from other natural entities runs through theological treatment of economics. Theology has too often participated in economics' focus on human needs to the exclusion of nature. This happened when theology adopted a dualistic separation of mind from body, spiritual from physical life. The result has been anti-materialism. Diatribes against materialism have shallowly thrown out the necessary and positive aspects of economics and our physicality along with its condemnation of excess and greed.[9]

This diatribe can be seen as resulting from the suspicion of flesh, of material things seducing the life of the spirit. However, let us stand that diatribe on its head a minute, and consider two other perspectives. First, Wendell Berry suggests that the religious community's preaching anti-materialism served historically to avoid the creation of an ethic governing the use of nature, the land, and our physical bodies.[10] What gets wiped out in this usage is the doctrine of creation interpreted as ongoing activities of the present, dynamic God. Another perspective comes from W.H. Auden who claims: "The great vice of Americans is not materialism but a lack of respect for matter."[11] Charles Cummings has referred to this as the "disenchantment of nature."[12]

This lack of respect for the material world, this veritable anti-materialism, becomes a very serious oversight when we realize that it creates a major distortion in the way we understand ourselves. We see ourselves as standing apart from nature, as burdened by our physicality, as creators and rulers rather than also creatures and coinhabitants. The lack of respect for nature, our own physical natures and the earth, meant that human well-being was too often identified as the totality of spiritual well-being. Economic conditions were considered less significant than spiritual ones. Two areas where the impact of this dichotomy has been great are the health of the land and the acquiescence of the church in economics' disregard of nature.

The stage has been set for the corrective theological recognition of our material home in economics. Contextual theologies of many kinds, but especially liberation theologies, have argued that one's context enters into theological beliefs. The environment is part of that context that cannot be forgotten. The church has been remiss in that it has often forgotten those in the forefront of environmental influence—farmers and rural residents. As a contextual theology of rural life develops, the connection between economics and ecology will become more visible for all of us.

2. The strangulation of our bodies. We have maintained that the earth is our home. The phytoplankton whose ability to absorb carbon emissions reduces the amount of ultraviolet radiation that we absorb is a graphic illustration of this. Similarly, our respiratory and gastrointestinal tracts receive some portion of the pollutants that our way of life produces.

The relationship between the way our economic system treats nature and the way it (we) treats our bodies is direct and incontrovertible. The connections "between the spirit and the body, the body and other bodies, the body and the earth," are indissolvable. "If these connections do necessarily exist . . . it is impossible, ultimately, to preserve ourselves apart from our willingness to preserve other creatures, or to respect and care for ourselves except as we respect and care for other creatures; and it is impossible to care for each other more or differently than we care for the earth."[13]

Economic System and Bodies. The advertising industry is integral to our economic system. That industry sells products and services by making us uneasy with our bodies and our psychic health, which it promises to assuage. Indeed, marketing is an activity directly tied into the manufacture and distribution of products. Our economy depends on any number of industries which are built by generating loathing for our own imperfect bodies. Examples that come to mind are the cosmetics, pharmaceuticals, health clubs, the food supply system, and travel industries.

The loathing of the body is also built into leisure activities. Barbara Ehrenreich wonders about the success of recent movies which "trash the body" with "eye gougings, power drilling" and other violent activities. She suggests there has always been a market for violence, as in the old-time western. "But," she says, "if offerings like *American Psycho* and *The Silence of the Lambs* (and *Terminator Two*) have anything to tell us about ourselves, it must be that at this particular historical moment, we have come to hate the body."[14]

These examples indicate a dynamic similar to that we identified earlier with regard to nature. If the standard of the health of nature is no longer the measure of economic systems, neither is our bodily health. We have externalized our own health from our economic system! Health has become something external to ourselves, something we buy at "health care centers" (formerly hospitals). Health is a private commodity that individuals buy at great private cost. Our agricultural system, part of the economy, turns food into waste products and our body into a consuming machine. Our bodies become something to manage, external to ourselves. Health is something we buy, not a basic standard which governs what products becomes available and are sold. Our bodies seem no longer to be under our control. One impact of this is a widespread sense of powerlessness, a failure to recognize that our bodily activity is itself a source of power.

Christian Disregard for Bodies. Little in the Christian faith, as recently enunciated, commends positive attention to our bodies. That this is so can be readily understood on the basis of our previous analysis. Nevertheless, this is shocking when seen in juxtaposition with some of the central tenets of the faith: the doctrine of creation, the incarnation of God in Jesus Christ. There **is** a long tradition of Christian concern with healing and bodily well-being, though we have compartmentalized that concern.

Rather, economics' disregard for the body has been joined all-too-comfortably with Christian paranoia about the body. James Nelson's work in *Embodiment* reveals, to the contrary, that regard for the body is central to Christian faith and can only be ignored to our detriment.[15] The body is a nemesis to asexual, disembodied theologies of sexuality. Similarly scripture has a continuous focus on God's concern for physical well-being.[16] We have spiritualized this biblical and theological theme. One effect of that has rendered salvation a matter of God's salvation of the individual spiritually, as though our souls were divisible from our bodies. I believe this emphasis has obscured many parts of our lives. Foremost among those are an appreciation of human sexuality and the material blessings of our lives.

Lost also is an awareness and acceptance of our limitations. Were we more aware of our limits we would be less subject to the dissatisfactions that our economy lives off of. We could attend more to the gifts that we do have, to the ways our physicality joins us with nature and other people, and to the ways our own health is tied to others'.

There are significant movements reintroducing us to our bodies. The women's movement, and feminist theology especially, has insisted that we pay attention to the way our bodies are a theological agenda. The church is beginning to accept healing and health care as being part of congregations' mission. With these and other movements reemphasizing the body as central to the human constitution, we hope to see a spirituality of the body. As this happens, the church will enunciate an alternative to the economy's externalization of the body. We will all be better for that, since we will then be called to an enjoyment and sharing of who we are. We will cease relentlessly pursuing what we cannot be.[17]

3. The strangulation of community. Here there is a very real divergence between economics' disregard for community and the current Christian emphasis on the corporate nature of life.

The Loss of Economic Community. The neoclassical economic system systematically obscures the fact that our home is a community. An economic system which focuses on the human individual not only writes off the environment, it even neglects the consequences of its activities for the human community. This is especially serious since it tends to reward negligence of the environment.

Neoclassical economics operates on a worldview which assumes that human beings are rational and self-interested. The purpose of human life is for individuals to pursue happiness freely. Thus, the ideal social world is a gathering of free individuals who compete with each other under conditions of scarcity to achieve self-interested goals.[18] Efficiency and growth are the engines of the economy. What remains unexamined is the relational character of life. It is simply assumed that individuals operating separately or even in corporations will produce the greatest good for the majority. On the basis of these assumptions the aggregate of individual goods swallows up the common good of the community. The result: an economy which reduces environmental impact to meeting EPA requirements. Those requirements are at odds with short-term efficiency and growth for the individual. This fosters a mentality which only strives to meet legal minimums.

The failure to address the ecological community derives from conceiving the economy as a closed system, "in which abstract exchange values circulate in a loop between production and consumption, in splendid isolation from the larger ecological system of which it is a part." This approach "neglects the general problems of aggregate (community) resource depletion and the limited capacity of natural systems to carry the macroeconomy as a whole."[19]

Christian Respect for Community. Christian believers can take comfort in our tradition's divergence from the disastrous oversight of our neoclassical economic system in this regard.[20] Throughout tradition there has been a strong emphasis on the community of the whole. To be sure, often community has been reduced to **human** community. Even there, however, what has prevented the Christian witness from neglecting the unity of the community of all life is belief in a sovereign God. As St. Thomas Aquinas put it, "The whole universe together participates in the divine goodness more perfectly, and represents it better than any single creature whatever."[21]

Even when emphasis on community has neglected to include the environment there has been a strong tradition of understanding nature as the book of creation. Hugh of St. Victor comments on Psalm 92:6 ("O Lord, how great are your works") that "The whole sensible world is like some book written by the finger of God, that is, created by divine power."[22]

This impulse toward the solidarity of nature within the human community will shape our recommendations for a Christian economic ecology. The range of beings that must be encompassed in any future Christian economic ethic will certainly include the health of the environment. The home whose future rests on economic care includes all of creation.

Economic Directions

At this point we can begin to articulate those remedial directions which could serve to guide our economic system. In the process we will be expanding the definition of economics to include precisely those entities which have previously been systematically excluded. However thoroughgoing our critique of the economic system's disregard of the environment, that should not blind us to two strengths. Those strengths are basically consonant with the Christian tradition.

1. The Value of the Human Individual. The U. S. system of economics has fostered a place for the individual. That the system has been overbalanced in this respect should not lead us to overlook its strengths. It has promoted a respect for the value of the individual. The system of legal rights has expressed the worth of each person. On the different basis of God's creation and unconditional love of all persons, the Christian tradition affirms the inherent dignity of persons. An environmental ethic should affirm the basic value of each person. It should not allow that value to be superseded by the value of other natural beings or abrogated in the name of the common good.[23]

2. Good Standard of Living. A second strength of our

modified capitalist system is its ability to produce goods and services which lead to a comfortable standard of living for most citizens. The ability to enjoy life with a decent standard of living is no mean feat, especially in comparison with many societies. This strength supports the Christian value of God's care for all as objects of his love and God's intention that we enjoy life. There is some consonance between this strength of the economic system and Christian tradition. A divergence occurs between the actual equality of concern that Christianity expresses and the inequality and suffering for some that results from economic practice. Nevertheless, we can affirm the freedom from want and the enjoyment that our economic system has generated for many.[24]

While we affirm these strengths, there are other outcomes that our economic system should remedy. We will express those as directions for future movement toward an economic system which respects our home.

3. An Economics which Connects. One of the clear directions that emerges from the previous discussion is simply that economics is broader than we in the United States conceive it. As Berry writes: "Our economy is based upon this disease [of disconnection]. Its aim is to separate us as far as possible from the sources of life (material, social, and spiritual), to put these sources under the control of corporations and specialized professionals, and to sell them to us at the highest profit."[25]

A first step toward reconnection involves our redefinition of economics so that it is not something external to us. Economics is not something out there that others control. Instead it involves everything from the way we spend our time and energies, to the way we relate to nature, to the way we relate to each other. It is the way we manage our lives, only one aspect of which involves money. Only one aspect of our lives involves production and consumption. We are not machines which produce and consume. We are human beings who work, who love, who appreciate, who enjoy. Sometimes it is hard to remember that.

4. Recovery of Nature. Central to our reconnection is the recovery of nature in counting economic costs and settling on future goals. That is vital to our remembering that we are physical, spatial, concretely spiritual creatures who must preserve the household we depend upon, that we are. The failure to take full account of the environment in our economic thinking is evidence of our mistaken belief that humankind can transcend its finitude. This is one source of sin and also of much distortion. We forget that we are natural and that we depend on nature.

Too often we leapfrog our legitimate dependencies and think **of ourselves** as those consumers whose "needs" and "desires" we need to fill. We think we can control our lives.[26] That also is a source of sin. Our sense of powerlessness derives from unrealistic expectations which are generated by our failure to remember that we are natural beings. We live with appetites unsatisfied and unsatisfiable, largely because we have written nature out of economic consideration. There have been disastrous results of ignoring environmental costs. The regeneration of home care demands home financing.

5. Recovery of Physical Selves. The ecologists have taught us that we cannot damage what we depend upon without damaging ourselves. Ignoring environmental impacts has accompanied ignoring our bodies. It is instructive that two other movements are gaining strength with the ecological one: the emphasis on wellness and fitness, and also the movement for nutritious safe foods. The notion of a healthy economy takes on new meaning as we connect our environment and our bodies. There are connections here to the work we do and the communities in which we live. Our lives are vocations that link us to the material world, that involve our bodies, and that tie us into community. To some degree. Too often our work is arranged in ways that take little account of our physicality. We may be unaware of that until our bodies rebel and we become sick. We can do much to care for our bodies, our selves.

6. The Recovery of Community. Our work-lives reveal our connection to the environment but also to our communities. The economic system which separates places of work and residence ignores our communities of relation. The economy of the Amish, in contrast, is organized around the question, "How will this economic decision affect the community?" This example makes vivid the absence of a communal factor in our dominant economic system. The fact that communal dynamics remain invisible in no way lessens their impact. Usually our economic relations operate in ways that lessen our integration into family, church, and civic associations. That leaves us feeling isolated, lonely, and independent of others. Our **relationships** have come to seem optional, and we wonder why our marital, parental, and public lives are so fragile!

Our economy has been delocalized. We in the rural community know this very well, as increasingly decisions which affect the local community are subject to distant corporations, government agencies, and expert professional policies. Local banks which once made loans partly on the basis of character are hemmed in by distant corporate policies. It is probably only that rural residents experience this more graphically than suburban or urban people.

As we come to the conclusion of this set of directions I am aware that it is not comprehensive. Rather, this set is an attempt to offer remedial directions. It can function, in dialogue with others, as goals toward a more wholistic economy.

The Economics of God

Our analysis to this juncture has demonstrated ways that the economic system has neglected central elements of who we are. It has contributed to the illness of our environment, to our psychic, spiritual and physical disease, and to the loss of communal relations. We have located remedial directions for an economics whose central agenda is the health of our planetary home.

What we need now is a theological perspective on the economy which incorporates these directions. We also need some practical directions or benchmarks for our economic activity. Thus, what is called for can be imaged as a small circle within a much larger one. The large circle represents nothing less than the kingdom of God. Obviously that kingdom includes an economics, and this economics will be an ideal for ecological life on this planet. It is—if you will—what God had in mind in creating us and all that is. The smaller circle is our economy, an economy which exists within the larger kingdom of God but which only partially resembles that ideal economy. It is our actual economy. The task of the ecologist and the Christian is to express moral directions and to act on them in such a way that the smaller circle comes more and more to resemble the larger.[27]

We will proceed by expressing five components of the vision of the larger circle—the economics of God. Then we will suggest several benchmarks or practicable ideals for our economic system. Those indicate ways in which elements of our economy could resemble the economics of the kingdom. These elements of the smaller circle will reflect our previous discussions as well.

A Sovereign Economics

The economics of God includes within its purview the entire cosmos. Everything that is has a place in God's economy. Not only does everything have a place, everything has its own place, its own value in itself. In creating the world, God affirmed the goodness of all created beings and also the whole of the created order. The upshot of this is that each individual being, each species, and the whole biosphere have God-given value. Each has both intrinsic and instrumental value. Economic life is comprehended within God's blueprint and should reflect God's sovereignty.

Benchmarks. The task set before us as human beings who exist in **an** economy is how to preserve and act in ways that allow all ecological begins to flourish. The following moral compass points express something of that vision:

1) Our economic system must be **redirected to include the well-being of all life**. That will necessitate attention to individual beings and the corporate whole.
2) Needed is a system of preserving or reclaiming **the rights of persons and all other species** which would maintain a minimal standard of justice. This will involve an expansion of the notion of rights now written into our political economy.
3) The system of rights will best be **held in tension with an economy which respects the genuine interests and well-being of all**. At a minimum this will

involve movement toward the guarantee of a "sufficiency."[28] The notion of a "sufficiency," which I am expanding to include ecospheric being, involves a modest **but secured** livelihood for all.

An Economics of *Shalom*

Within the theological vision of God's home, we see not only the goodness of each being, but that everything is related to everything else in a divine ecology, a unity of all in **shalom**. There is one commonwealth, one community, one kingdom, one economy. Everything is connected to all else. We depend for our well-being upon God's creating, sustaining, and re-deeming activity in all other natural processes. Other life-forms depend similarly on God's activity in all other beings. The vision is of genuine interdependence, that each being contributes its distinctive gifts to the wellness of the whole.

Benchmarks. Within the larger circle of **shalom**, which is only fully realizable in the kingdom, there are benchmarks which begin to express that moral vision. Clearly **shalom** catches up at least one of the sovereign God's central purposes in creation. The goal of structuring an economy for unified well-being would fundamentally alter every known economic system. These benchmarks capture some intermediate steps toward that wholeness.

4)[29] Our economic system **should address** as a cen-tral priority **the gap that exists between rich and poor**. No part of our society can rest content until the suffering and illness that arise from economic maldistribution is addressed and ameliorated. Without that remediation, other moves toward economic unity are doomed.

5) **All biospheric life** is valuable and **deserves consideration**, e.g., legal standing. The goal of legal and moral consideration aims at **equality of standing.** This would help determine the requirements for ecological renewability and sustainability.

6) The basic dynamic of economic life must change toward **communitarian rather than individual benefit.** At present our basing an economy on **costly choice** and scarcity leads to an ever-widening appropriation of nature and human resources (people). Growth has become our goal. Rather, **economic health should be measured in terms of expanding the enjoyment and quality of life** available to **all** persons and species.[30]

7) What must not be overlooked is **the necessity of community-wide participation in economic decision making.** Other species must have a voice in that process—perhaps through a system of significant incentives and community/consumer sanctions.

At this point I have to remind myself that this chapter is illustrative, not exhaustive. There are many other benchmarks or middle axioms that could, even should, be developed. Some of those result from other elements of the theological vision.

An Economy of Divine Presence

Theology is putting positive emphasis on the real active **presence** of God in the life of the world today. Renewed emphasis on God's presence is breaking down a hierarchical separation of human species from others. This will bring our human intentions and values into perspective.

The theological vision of divine presence lifts economics out of its autonomy. It ennobles economics, and suggests that economics in fact embodies God's presence already. That it can more completely do so is the object of our moral benchmarks.

Benchmarks. Shalom and presence are both evidenced in the doctrine of the Trinity. We image God through that doctrine as a community of persons, each being variously present in the world. If we take this image as the larger circle directing our economic ecology, we discover that the norms appropriate to that vision influence economic life.[31] We will limit ourselves to considering three areas of economic life in this section: the world of nature, work, and property.

8) Were our economic system to reflect God's presence in nature, **it would take the conservation, preservation, and careful usage of all species, humankind included, far more seriously**. The belief in divine presence operating throughout the world would discourage dichotomous thinking. It would encourage efforts toward harmonious and symbiotic care.

9) If our system perceived God to be present in work, then the **nature of that work would reflect the value of each worker**. It would also reflect the contribution the worker makes to the community, and the responsible relating of that work to God, others, and nature. The workplace would exhibit shared authority and access to power.[32] It would reflect ecologically sustainable conditions.

10) God's presence in the world suggests a view of

property as a communal gift to be shared. Even if property is best held by individuals, it is a means of grace whereby God blesses us to share with others. Rather than a commodity to be hoarded, it is a common inheritance upon which all biospheric beings have a call. This expands upon traditional, though forgotten, enunciations of the Torah, Augustine, and Thomas.[33]

The vision of God's presence has wide impact, especially upon the way in which we perceive the economy. This is terribly significant, since it breaks the logjam which has separated theology and economics.

An Economy of Transcendent Purpose

Christians affirm as the first article of their faith a belief in God's being the creator of the universe. We also believe that God sustains the whole creation and continues the work of creativity. Two of the ways God works are through human agency and divine providence. God works through human agents, through the church, and through nature in ways that express gracious purpose. God provides in accord with God's will for ecological well-being.

Part of the wider vision here is that God's economy expresses a transcendent purpose. What this purpose implies is that our economy is accountable to actualize God's intentions. It is not purposeless or arbitrary in its directions. It should reflect God's gracious goals for ecospheric health.

Benchmarks. In a sense all aspects of an ethic of ecology can be seen as a corollary of God's transcendent purpose. The impact of this fourth feature of God's economy is to hold human beings accountable in **their considerable power** to **God's purpose and power**. We are reminded both of God's transcendence expressed in human partnership and also of human finitude, both agency and sin.

11) There is a **presumption against intervening** in beneficent natural processes **only for human benefit**. What we know of human sinfulness and limitation makes us wary of our own motives and perspective. We are called to live within our limits, to see them as "graced" rather than a challenge to overcome.

12) Likewise, this suggests that **only highly significant purposes justify ecological interventions that are irreversible**. Humility, caution, and conservation are ecologically appropriate in light of God's purposes.

Human agents, and especially the church, are called to discern God's purposes and to recover an economy that expresses them. As an economy comes closer to actualizing God's purpose, it will also come closer to supporting the life of the whole planet.[34]

Economics and Righteousness

The economy of God is a production and distribution of goods and services in accord with God's righteousness. Our home was created and is to be governed in accord with God's being. Righteousness is the expression of that being, God's "steadfast love, justice, righteousness in the earth" (Jer 9:24). It is God's design for right relations between beings. Not narrowly moralistic, the term "righteousness" refers to the core of how God relates to the world. First, acting in self-giving love, God also acts justly and then mercifully. Meeks equates this righteousness with God's "power for life" and ability to liberate life.[35] There is a struggle going on between those things that exhibit righteousness and those that pull our home towards destruction.

Benchmarks. We human beings are called to exemplify God's righteousness in our economic dealings. This is a call to right relations with each other, natural life, and God. From among the range of guideposts that could be included in the smaller circle, we select these three:

13) An economic system **should promote the wholeness of all parts of creation**, because the promotion of any part builds up the harmony and joy of every other.[36] **Economic analysis should be wholistic** in taking the health of all ecosystems and the impact of activities on the total ecospheric functioning into account.

14) **Justice**, in this vision, **becomes a matter of hungering and thirsting after right relations**. Acting toward the health of all fulfills the lust for consumption that does not satisfy. It is a way of satisfying and enjoying ourselves as well as sharing sufficiently so that other beings can enjoy and be satisfied.

15) An economic system should be designed in such a way as to sustain the well-being of all within that system. **Sustainability thus becomes a key measure of justice**. In our present situation, restoring the system to sustainability or, better, **regenerativity** may be what is implied by this axiom. Our system should aim at healing those relations which have been broken.

Conclusion

At this point our testing of the theoretical position developed in chapters 1 through 6 is complete. While there are still many areas that could be investigated, it is clear that the position offers distinctive moral directions. It does so in both the difficult and vital area of economic life.

These directions are not the same as public policy. That step remains for others to make. It is an essential step but it is outside the purview of this book. There is one step that must be outlined in abbreviated fashion. That is the step toward action. It is not enough to leave the health of our home up to governmental action. We as individuals and church members have the privilege of acting in ways that will transform our society more and more into God's home—and ours.

Epilogue

The remains of several hundred giant statues seem to have been erected as sentries around tiny Easter Island. They failed, however, to protect the island from its own inhabitants. At the height of its civilization there were apparently 8,000 residents of the island living in a two-class society which was entirely dependent on its own resources. It was then that the statues were erected. The climate and location of Easter Island would lead one to expect a pleasant landscape with varied vegetation. And so it was.

Apparently the demands of the growing population on its trees led to their being stripped off the thin soil of the volcanic island. Erosion followed. The combination of erosion, drought, and the oppressive orders of the ruling elite led to a civil war around 1678. The elite were destroyed; anarchy prevailed; cannibalism became widespread. Then, around 1860, Peruvian ships carried off all the leaders of the community to be sold as slaves. Reports from later visits by European ships evoke great pity. One described the island as a bone yard, the statues lying toppled on their faces, the landscape barren and treeless.

I recount this history as a parable of what could happen to our Easter Island. Our home could experience this intermixture of social violence and ecological insensitivity. There is a bright side to this story. The islanders and the Chilean government, with aid from the United States, are undertaking the rebirth of the forests on the island. There is real hope that the land that had been decimated can be returned to health and fertility. As the first trees take hold they attract birds that help disseminate seeds. A positive spiral of cause and effect promises the resurrection of the variety and beauty of Easter Island.[1]

We Are Involved

Several things have struck me over and over again in the course of researching and writing this book. One is the simple fact that whether we like it or not we are involved in the future of the environment. We are part and parcel of our home. Our actions have consequences. We are not immune or separate from the environment. We are it. It is us. That is just so clear, so overwhelming, that it is almost incredible to me that we could somehow have thought of ourselves as separate from nature. We **are** going to act in ways that affect the quality of **our** island. The question is what sort of impact we will have.

A second thing that kept gaining force as the book continued was the power of recognizing our **bodily** life. Maybe women have known this in more starkly visceral ways than men. The insight that we are embodied in space and time has far-flung ramifications. One is that my future is tied up with that of other bodily creatures, whether they be animal like myself, or plant. We share embodiment. The depletion of the ozone layer will affect us in roughly similar ways.

What this also seems to mean is that there will be no solution to environmental disease that does not also address issues of social justice. The health of the environment and the quality of people's lives are such interconnected issues that the two will improve or decline together.

Recognizing my embodiment also throws into experiential question my academic status as critical analyst. It is hard to maintain cognitive distance as an intellectually tenable position any more. Even for heuristic purposes, assuming distance from the environment generates misconceptions and insensitivity. Finally, and before I get too carried away, my/our being embodied creatures means that I/we have power. We can act. We are not omnipotent, but each of us has power. Together we have a lot of power.

A third thing that seems to emerge out of the first two is that we can best begin dealing with problems of eco-justice right where we are. What I am suggesting is that we too easily get immobilized by the scope and immensity, for example, of worldwide warming. What we need to do instead is to find out first what our local ecology is. How does our municipal garbage get incinerated? How does it get disposed of? What is the future of our landfill? We can do something to improve the quality of the ecology of our local neighborhood. Being able to improve the local ecology contributes to global ecology. It also strengthens us to act regionally and nationally.

The intention of this epilogue then is simply to catalog a few ways that we as individuals and as the Christian church can act to regenerate our homeplanet, our Easter Island. My hope is that these will serve to stimulate appropriate activities in your neighborhood.

Steps Toward Home

I have surveyed a multitude of lists of recommended "ways to save the planet."[2] Those suggestions seem to fall into several categories: worship, education, life-style, home, institutions, and politics. I will use those categories to organize some recommendations both for individual and church activities. It is important that actions of individual Christians be reinforced and furthered by the church acting corporately. Local churches, national churches, and the worldwide body of Christ can act in concert to renew the earth.

Worship. If God is present in creation, our worship should reflect God's presence. Ecology will only become central to the theology and life of the church as the environment becomes a regular part of worship. Thus it is important to incorporate concern for creation into every worship service. The eucharist, Lord's supper, and baptism are sacramental occasions when natural products are integral to worship. Opening calls to worship and prayers of adoration are opportune and regular occasions for honoring God's earth.

Corporate worship could place more emphasis on the world as God's home. Sermons and homilies can be sensitive to the physical and natural components of scripture. Those who develop liturgical resources can draw together creation-centered hymns, prayers, and other resources.[3] In addition, parts of the creation—plants regularly, animals sometimes—could be brought into the sanctuary. Moreover, the congregation could worship outside several times during a year. Anything that emphasizes our physical oneness with the rest of the world in a public way helpfully reflects the unity of our homeplace.

Worship is also an individual act that expresses our devotion to God. As individuals we could learn to worship God by enjoying the world and our bodily selves, by taking walks or caring for our local habitat.

Education. The task of educating ourselves and others is a continuous process which takes place in formal and informal situations. Maybe the first step is simply to get outdoors and enjoy it. As individuals we can continue to educate ourselves, our children, and other groups into the wonders and dynamics of the environment. Such processes might also include investigating farming practices, industrial waste disposal, and local water treatment facilities. We could plant individual and congregational gardens, harvest and eat the food we grow there.

Our churches have a "special role in environmental matters," according to Russell E. Train. The church may not have the technical expertise to enter complex debates over environmental issues, but he says, however, that "it does have the credibility and the historic mission of articulating and teaching values to society."[4] The church can do this in many ways, ranging from Sunday morning classes, to arranging its own life in ecologically responsible ways, to political advocacy. Urban and rural churches could form educational partnerships toward greater awareness.

Life-styles. Our life-styles reflect the attitudes we have learned socially. It is also true that life-style changes can change attitudes. This is clearly an area where we do have power. Some of the changes we can make are in the area of what we buy. Thus we can avoid cosmetics and household products whose testing involves cruelty to animals. We can buy clothing that respects animal life. We can eat foods that are organically grown and are low in fat, cholesterol, and calories. We can reuse mugs rather than styrofoam.[5] We can patronize restaurants and buy products that are eliminating waste packaging.

Our local and national churches can practice many of the same suggestions. Modelling nutritious and ecologically sound practices at church is educational. Congregation members could have a potluck food fair at which everyone shared one recipe and one recycling idea. A church could find out how the food it buys locally or at the grocery store is grown and transported.

Home. We are thinking in this section about the residences we inhabit. How do we as individuals or families heat and cool our homes? We could lower the thermostats during the winter and raise them during the summer. Making those changes gradually will be barely perceptible, so adaptive are our bodies.

As churches and church members we can lower the settings on our water heaters or install automatic timers on them. We can let the sunshine warm our homes and churches. We can wait to run dishwashers or washing machines until they are full. We can pay attention to recycling codes. The church I attend has a different family wash coffee cups after worship each week, a practice which encourages good conservation in all the people who attend.

Institutions. Environmental quality rises or falls with institutional, as well as personal, care. Individual leaders within institutions have significant clout as they live out their vocations in an environmentally alert fashion. Production, distribution, inter-office, and external relations are all institutional functions with ecological impact. Individuals can support local institutions and, in supporting them, suggest that they raise their level of environmental responsibility. As leaders get involved with others in different institutions we can work together toward greater sustainability.

Churches can become involved with other social institutions. For example, some churches have pressed for regenerative agricultural practices. Others have helped set up farmers' markets. Others work for community development in rural areas. In their efforts to promote better health care,[6] churches can direct attention to better nutrition and environmentally sound health practices. The connections between human and biospheric health make us aware of our bondedness in community.

Politics. Besides other activities there are political ones. By that I mean the levels of local and state as well as federal government.[7] Usually federal initiatives follow local ones. Individuals can be particularly effective at influencing local decisions. We can, for example, press for curbside recycling. These efforts will be effective, particularly if that can be shown to relieve pressure on local budgets. We can lobby for glass and aluminum recycling laws. We can press for fee structures that reward recycling; the less you throw away, the less you pay. We can press for greater fuel efficiency and lower operating costs for automobiles.

As national churches, many Catholic and Protestant bodies support advocacy groups which lobby for ecologically wise public policy: The National and World Councils of Churches, Bread for the World, National Catholic Rural Life Committee, Church World Relief, and individual denominational offices. There are other organizations whose offices aim at state—or region-wide influence—PrairieFire, the Land Stewardship Project, the Center for Rural Affairs, and the Commission on Religion in Appalachia. Join the local chapter of the Audubon Society or the Sierra Club as a church.

The church itself is a political as well as a spiritual and economic institution which shapes environmental attitudes and practices. It is the voluntary organization with the greatest promise for regenerating the planet.

We need Christian congregations who understand that God is present in the world, who see that the incarnation of Jesus Christ revealed our bodies and our world to be God's home, who understand that the Spirit is still moving over the face of the deep. Indeed, who live out the understanding that we are home.

Notes

Preface

1. Hildevert of Lavardin, quoted in Kenneth L. Gibble, "Hometowns and Holy Ground," *Presbyterian Survey*, April 1991, p. 24.

2. John Roach, in a summary of "Moral Dimension of Environmental Problems," a Scriptural and Theological Consultation, cosponsored by the U.S. Catholic Conference and the Catholic University of America, November 30–December 1, 1990, p. 2. Many participants at the conference sounded the same theme.

3. See Robin Broad, John Cavanagh, and Walden Bello, "Development: The Market Is Not Enough," *Foreign Policy* 81 (Winter 1990–1991), pp. 144–162. See also Jack Nelson-Pallmeyer, *Brave New World Order* (Maryknoll, N.Y.:Orbis Books, 1992), especially Chapter Seven on "Environmental Disorder."

4. Msgr. Charles Murphy made claims similar to this at the U.S. Catholic Conference, "Moral Dimensions of Environmental Problems," Consultation, quoted above, p. 6.

5. Two helpful resources are: David H. Fisher, "The Role of Aesthetic Images in Moral and Ethical Reflection," a paper presented at the American Academy of Religion annual convention, Kansas City, November 1991, and S. Dennis Ford, *Sins of Omission: A Primer on Moral Indifference* (Minneapolis: Augsburg Fortress, 1990).

1. Where We Are: Our Home

1. Charles Birch, "The Scientific-Environmental Crisis: Where Do the Churches Stand?" *The Ecumenical Review* 40:2, April 1988, p. 189. See also Ken Wilber, *The Holographic Paradigm and Other Paradoxes* (Berkeley: Shambhala Publications, 1988), p. 250.

2. Robert Kunzig, "Invisible Garden," *Discover*, April 1990, pp. 67–74. My treatment of "plankters" comes from this account.

3. Ibid., p. 68.

4. Ibid., pp. 72–73.

5. Eric Skjei and M. Donald Whorton, *Of Mice and Molecules: Technology and Human Survival* (New York: Dial Press, 1983), p. 19.

6. UNEP/GEMS, "The Greenhouse Gases" (Nairobi: United Nations Environment Programme, 1987), quoted by Gerald Barney, "The Physical Environment," The Year 2000 and Beyond Conference, ELCA, unpublished paper, p. 6.

7. Ibid.

8. Lester Brown, et al., *The State of the World 1989* (New York: W.W. Norton & Company, 1989), p. 9. See also Hilary F. French, "Strengthening Global Environmental Goverance," in Brown, ed., *State of the World 1992*, pp. 159–161.

9. On the way this effect is creeping northward to Chile, see "Life Under the Ozone Hole," in *Time*, December 9, 1991, p. 43.

10. For a far more extensive treatment of this see Cynthia Pollock

Shea, "Protecting the Ozone Layer" in Lester Brown, *State of the World 1989*, pp. 77–79.

11. Barney, pp. 9–10. His timeline is two generations.

12. Ibid.

13. Skjei and Whorton, *Of Mice and Molecules*, p. 1.

2. How Did We Get Here?

1. Jonathan Schell, *The Fate of the Earth* (New York: Alfred A. Knopf, 1982).

2. Teilhard de Chardin, *The Phenomenon of Man* (revised ed.; New York: Harper, 1965), pp. 254–311. See Conrad Bonifazi, "Teilhard and the Natural Environment," in Philip N. Joranson and Ken Butigan, eds. *Cry of the Environment* (Santa Fe: Bear & Company, 1984).

3. Some of the tactics of the Earth First! organization come across as almost anti-human. See S. Talbot, "Earth First! What Next?," *Mother Jones* 15:6 (November/December 1990), or B. Carpenter, "Redwood Radicals," *U.S. News and World Report* 109 (September 17, 1990).

4. If we need a date, I believe 1950 is a good candidate. The population of the planet, and the demands made upon the planet's resources, have more than doubled since then.

5. J. Donald Hughes, in his book *Ecology in Ancient Civilizations* (Albuquerque: University of New Mexico Press, 1975) speaks of the admirable Greek and Roman land ethic in antiquity. The deforestation of the Greek islands during classical times contrasts sharply with the voices of Plato and others during that period who called for

care of the land. A discrepancy existed between ideal and practice. It is as though one took the beauty of natural landscape photographs in a Sierra Club magazine as mirroring contemporary conditions and prevalent attitudes.

6. Robert Bellah, Richard Madsen, William M. Sullivan, Ann Swidler, and Steven M. Tipton, *Habits of the Heart: Individualism and Commitment in American Life* (Berkeley: University of California Press, 1985).

7. Tex Sample, *U.S. Lifestyles and Mainline Churches* (Philadelphia: Westminster/John Knox Press, 1990).

8. Gibson Winter, *Community and Spiritual Transformation: Religion and Politics in a Communal Age* (New York: Crossroad, 1989). Winston Persaud helped me understand that there are communities that we belong to involuntarily. The ecological community is one of those.

9. Paul G. King, Kent Maynard, and David O. Woodyard, *Risking Liberation: Middle Class Powerlessness and Social Heroism* (Atlanta: John Knox Press, 1988).

10. Quoted in Wesley Granberg-Michaelson, *Ecology and Life: Accepting Our Environmental Responsibility* (Waco, TX: Word Books, 1988), p. 23.

11. Alan B. Durning, "Junk Food, Food Junk," *World Watch* 4:5, September-October 1991, pp. 7–9. "Junk food leads to high blood pressure, heart disease, obesity, and diabetes, while generating mountains of waste and absorbing surprising quantities of energy and materials."

12. See Paul L. Wachtel, *The Poverty of Affluence: A Psychological Portrait of the American Way of Life* (Philadelphia: New Society Publishers, 1989), esp. 1–55. Wachtel's view is that we have sought

to find happiness in consumption rather than in communal bonds, a futile effort.

13. On this point see E.F. Schumacker, *Small Is Beautiful: Economics as If People Mattered* (New York: Harper & Row, 1975); John Kenneth Galbraith, "The Dependence Effect," in Tom L. Beauchamp and Norman E. Bowie, eds. *Ethical Theory and Business* (Englewood Cliffs, N. J.: Prentice-Hall, Inc., 1979), pp. 498–501. Garrett Hardin's well-known parable of the commons makes a similar point.

14. See Prentiss L. Pemberton and David Rush Finn, *Towards a Christian Economic Ethic: Stewardship and Social Power* (Minneapolis: Winston Press, 1985). They make the point that the value of efficiency is at base an individualistic, rather than a corporate, one.

15. I have written a number of pieces indicating the widespread impact of this transcendent dualism and suggesting a way of overcoming it. See my "Ethics, Agriculture, and the Material Universe," *The Annual of the Society of Christian Ethics 1986*, Alan B. Anderson, ed. (Washington: Georgetown University Press, 1987), pp. 219–250. See also James B. Nelson, *Embodiment: An Approach to Sexuality and Christian Theology* (Minneapolis: Augsburg Publishing House, 1978).

16. Wesley Granberg-Michaelson, *Ecology and Life*, p. 35.

17. James M. Gustafson, *Ethics from a Theocentric Perspective* I (Chicago: University of Chicago Press, 1981), pp. 272–273.

18. See Shannon Jung, "Feminism and Spatiality: Ethics and the Recovery of a Hidden Dimension," *Journal of Feminist Studies in Religion* 4:1 (Spring 1988), pp. 55–72.

19. Ivor Leclerc, *The Nature of Physical Existence* (London: George Allen & Unwin, Ltd., 1972), p. 314, *passim*.

20. Contemporary *scientists* have again become interested in cos-mological and theological questions; it is their work—rather than that of theologians—which has pressed them in that direction.

21. I refer primarily to the classic essay, reprinted *ad nauseam*, of Lynn White, Jr., "The Historical Roots of Our Ecological Crisis," first printed in *Science*. Vol. 155, March 10, 1967, pp. 1203–1207. On this topic see my "The Recovery of the Land: Agribusiness and Creation-Centered Stewardship" in Rowland A. Sherrill, ed. *Religion and the Life of the Nation: American Recoveries* (Urbana, IL: University of Illinois Press, 1990) and my "Agricultural Technology As If God Were Involved," *Reformed Review* 41:3 (Spring 1988).

22. Stephen Toulmin, "Nature and Nature's God," *Journal of Religious Ethics* 13:1 (Spring 1985), p. 42. Bracketed material represents a correlation that Toulmin makes on the next page.

23. Ibid., p. 43.

24. Charles West courageously quotes some of his own past writing to indicate this trend. "The biblical story," he *had* written,

> . . . also secularizes nature. It places creation—the physi-cal world—in the context of the covenant relation and does not try to understand it apart from that relation. The history of God with his people has a setting, and this set-ting is created nature. But the movement of history, not the structure of the setting, is central to reality . . . The physical world, in other words, does not have its meaning in itself. There are no spirits at work in it which can help or harm mankind. It is the creation of God and the object of his manipulation. ["God-Woman/Man-Creation," *The Ecumenical Review* 33:1 (January 1981), p. 26, citing works from 1959 and 1966.]

Evident also in West's quote is the peculiar exclusion of God's activity in *history* from the whole realm of nature. The enervation of the force of nature from history (Consider the historic effect of the very material atomic bomb, for example!) is probably a result of the affinity between a sin-salvation *Heilsgeschichte* interpretation of the Bible and the eschatological pull toward the final days.

25. Ibid, p. 26.

3. Why the Health of the Environment Is a Spiritual Issue

1. Karen J. Warren, "The Power and the Promise of Eco-feminism," *Environmental Ethics* 12:2 (Summer 1990), pp. 134–135.

2. John Muir, *To Yosemite and Beyond: Writings from the Years 1863 to 1875*, ed. Robert Engsberg and Donald Wesling (Madison: University of Wisconsin Press, 1980), pp. 145–146.

3. Richard Cartwright Austin, *Baptized into Wilderness: A Christian Perspective on John Muir* (Atlanta: John Knox Press, 1987), helps us see the connections between Muir's faith and Christianity, but also enables us to understand Muir's hostility to Christianity.

4. H. Richard Niebuhr, "The Center of Value," in *Radical Monotheism and Western Culture* (London: Faber and Faber, 1961), p.105.

5. Luther Standing Bear, *Land of the Spotted Eagle* (Lincoln: University of Nebraska Press, 1933), p. 45.

6. See Rosemary Radford Ruether, *Womanguides: Readings toward a Feminist Theology* (Boston: Beacon Press, 1985), Chapter Three.

7. Muir, *To Yosemite and Beyond*, p. 69.

8. Sigmund Freud, *Civilization and Its Discontents*, in James Strachey, trans., *The Complete Psychological Works of Sigmund Freud*, Vol. XXI, (London: The Hogarth Press, 1961), p. 64.

9. Ibid., p. 72.

10. John Muir, "Wild Wool," *Wilderness Essays* (Salt Lake City: Peregrine Smith, Inc., 1980), p. 228.

11. Aldo Leopold, *A Sand County Almanac* (New York: Ballantine Books, 1966), p. 251. The two essays referred to can be found on pp. 188–201 and 226–233.

12. Ibid., p. 239.

13. Ibid., p. 262.

14. This section on beauty benefitted from the insights of Richard Cartwright Austin, "Beauty: A Foundation for Environmental Ethics," *Environmental Ethics* 7:3 (Fall 1985), pp. 197–208.

15. Bill Devall and George Sessions, *Deep Ecology: Living as If Nature Mattered* (Salt Lake City: Gibbs M. Smith, 1985), p. 70. Arne Naess has been a key leader of this movement.

16. The strongest claim I have located is Karen J. Warren's essay in *Environmental Ethics*. However, there are many others—Carol P. Christ, Judith Plant, Carolyn Merchant, Elizabeth Dodson Gray, Susan Griffin, Katherine Davis, Iris Young, and a multitude of others—who make similar claims. I will include here only those feminists who are not explicitly Christian, since this chapter has bracketed Christian reasons for ecological concern. That has excluded from mention such strong voices as Sallie McFague, Virginia Stem Owens, and Rosemary Radford Ruether. Nor have I

included perspectives from any non-Christian, "formal" religious thinkers—Buddhist, Taoist, Hindu, or Jewish.

17. Carol P. Christ, "Rethinking Theology and Nature," in Judith Plaskow and Carol Christ, eds. *Weaving the Vision: New Patterns in Feminist Spirituality* (San Francisco: Harper & Row, 1989), p. 314.

18. Ibid. These "ancient and traditional views" may have been more ideal than actual, of course.

19. Susan Griffin, *Women and Nature: The Roaring Inside Her* (New York: Harper & Row, 1978), p. 227.

20. See my essay on "Feminism and Spatiality" arguing that women have been more in tune with their spatiality, and that the distinctive strengths of women's experience should inform contemporary ethics.

21. Alice Walker, *The Color Purple* (New York: Pocket Books, 1982), pp. 178–179.

22. Warren, p. 125.

23. Warren, pp. 139–145.

4. The Earth: God's Home, Our Home

1. William Temple, *Nature, Man, and God* (London: MacMillan and Co., 1935), p. 478.

2. It is also impossible to read or interpret scripture as though it were produced in a cultural vacuum or that it could ever be read by a generic someone, an "empty" person without cultural background or faith presuppositions. It is impossible to read scripture without being in a hermeneutic circle, i.e., we always bring our own ques-

tions and freight to the text. Thus, theology, interpreting the biblical text from within our own frame of reference and context, is always going on when we talk about biblical meaning. Another way of saying this is that there is a surplus of meaning; the categories of the Bible are not hermetically sealed off from our lives. We bring our lives to the text and the text to our lives.

3. Richard Cartwright Austin, *Hope for the Land: Nature in the Bible* (Atlanta: John Knox Press, 1988), pp. 43–50.

4. Jurgën Moltmann, *God In Creation: A New Theology of Creation and the Spirit of God* (San Francisco: Harper & Row, 1985).

5. I fully believe that an earth-sensitive reading of scripture would produce an ecologically more profound interpretation of scripture such as feminist revisionism has produced for women.

6. James Gustafson, *Ethics from a Theocentric Perspective*, Vol. I. (Chicago: University of Chicago Press, 1981), p. 251.

7. See Walter Brueggemann, "Theodicy in a Social Dimension," *Journal for the Study of the Old Testament* 33:3 (October 1985). Brueggemann makes the case that the problem of evil in the Old Testament is linked both with social process and with God, as well as with natural, moral and religious dimensions.

8. See Job 38:39–41, 39:29–30; Psalm 104:21, 136:25, 147:9; Amos 3:4. Examples of pastoral imagery abound, from Nathan's rebuke to David (2 Sam 11:1–12:7;) to Jesus' parable of the good shepherd (Mt 18:12–14; Lk 15:3–7; Jn 10:1–18, 26–28). George L. Frear, Jr. provides a cornucopia of *biblical* images pointing to God's "Caring for Animals: Biblical Stimulus for Ethical Reflection," in Jay McDaniel and Charles Pinches, *Good News for Animals?* (New York: Orbis Books, forthcoming).

9. On this point, see Paul Santmire, *The Travail of Nature: The*

Ambiguous Ecological Promise of Christian Theology (Philadelphia: Fortress Press, 1985), *passim* but esp. pp. 183–189.

10. It is useful for us to note that the Bible stretches our understandings of home in ways that are consistent with, but push beyond, popular conceptions.

11. See the very helpful essay by William C. French, "Ecological Concerns and the Anti-Foundationalist Debate: James Gustafson on Biospheric Constraints" in D.M. Yeager, ed., *The Annual of the Society of Christian Ethics 1989* (Washington, D.C.: Georgetown University Press, 1989), pp.113–130.

12. This school of thought is associated with a number of prominent biblical scholars, especially Gerhard von Rad and George Ernest Wright. That school understands scripture primarily as a series of covenants and acts of God. This lends a crisis mentality to scripture, an emphasis with some affinity to twentieth century events and with history.

Liberation theology, in some ways very different from *Heilsgeschichte* interpretations, shares with them an emphasis on historical as opposed to natural categories, kairotic moments, a crisis mentality, and emphasis on *some* biblical events—deliverance, exodus, exile.

My point is not, of course, to deny the validity of these events or emphases. It is to suggest an overemphasis on the discontinuous, the singular event, and the historical to the neglect of the continuous, the routine conditions and activities, the natural, and the physical.

13. Claus Westermann, *Elements of Old Testament Theology* (Atlanta, GA: John Knox Press, 1982), p. 103.

14. See Gustafson, *Ethics From A Theocentric Perspective*, I, especially Chapter 5, and also the issue studies in *Ethics . . .*, II.

15. Beverly Wildung Harrison, "The Power of Anger in the Work

of Love: Christian Ethics for Women and Other Strangers," *Union Seminary Quarterly Review* 36 (Supplementary, 1981), pp. 48–49.

16. See Santmire, "The Future of the Cosmos and the Renewal of the Church's Life with Nature," in Ted Peters, ed. *Cosmos as Creation* (Nashville, TN: Abingdon Press, 1989), p. 275. Santmire suggests there that "the earth is cursed by humanity's sinfulness," but that "nature in itself is not fallen. The notion of a cosmic fall is essentially extrabiblical."

5. Being Ourselves: The Human–Nature Relationship

1. Bill French correctly warns us against assuming that "a turn to nature and creation entails a turn away from culture and history." See his "Ecological Concern and the Anti-Foundationalist Debates: James Gustafson on Biospheric Constraints," in *The Annual of the Society of Christian Ethics 1989*, p. 113.

2. For an overview of the creation-centered tradition and its four "ways" or "paths," including the mystic, see Matthew Fox, *Original Blessing* (Sante Fe, New Mexico: Bear & Company, 1983).

3. Richard Lang, "The Dwelling Door: Towards a Phenomenology of Transition," in David Seamon and Robert Mugerauer, eds. *Dwelling, Place and Environment: Toward a Phenomenology of Person and World* (New York: Columbia University Press, 1985), p. 201. This work is basically an extension and exposition of Martin Heidegger's essay "Building Dwelling Thinking," in Heidegger, *Basic Writings* (San Francisco: Harper, 1977), pp. 319–340.

4. "Building Dwelling Thinking," Ibid.

5. Seamon, "Reconciling Old and New Worlds: The Dwelling-Journey Relationship as Portrayed in Vilhelm Moberg's 'Emigrant' Novels," in Seamon and Mugerauer, eds., p. 243. One wonders how

Heidegger might analyze the widespread homelessness in the United States today.

6. Zimmerman, "The Role of Spiritual Discipline in Learning to Dwell On Earth," in Seamon and Mugerauer, p. 249.

7. Wendell Berry, "Waste," in *What Are People For?* (San Francisco: North Point Press, 1990), p. 127.

8. Hans Jonas, *The Phenomenon of Life: Towards a Philosophical Biology* (Chicago: The University of Chicago Press, 1966), p. 215. (Bracketed material added.)

9. French, p. 122.

10. See, e.g., Edward T. Hall, *The Hidden Dimension* (Garden City, N.Y.: Doubleday, 1966).

11. For a more complete theoretical description of what is involved in those terms, see my article "Spatiality, Relativism, and Authority," *Journal of the American Academy of Religion* L:2 (June 1982), 215–235, which offers an anatomy of spatiality.

12. See, e.g., Charles Cummings, *Eco-Spirituality: Toward A Reverent Life* (Mahwah, NJ: Paulist Press, 1991).

13. J. Edward Tether, "Brain," *Encyclopedia Americana,* Vol. IV, (Danbury, CT: Grolier Incorporated, 1988), pp. 420–421.

14. Robert Ornstein and Richard F. Thompson, *The Amazing Brain* (Boston: Houghton Mifflin, 1984), pp. 92–95.

15. Ibid. p. 154. In a further linkage of mind and nature, Ornstein and Thompson suggest that "the fresh air of mountain tops, waterfalls, and other places where the ion concentration is greater" may

have an objective, positive effect on brain development. See pp. 167–168.

16. "Brain," *Encyclopedia Americana*, p. 421.

17. Stephen Toulmin and June Goodfield, *The Architecture of Matter* (New York: Harper & Row, 1966), p. 375.

18. Ibid.

19. I have argued the co-implication of identity and also the interdependence of self-regard and other-regard in an article, "Autonomy as Justice: Spatiality and the Revelation of Otherness," *Journal of Religious Ethics* 14:1 (Spring 1986), pp. 157–183.

20. This is Gary Comstock's description as found in a study by E.S.E. Hafez and J.P. Signoret, "The Behavior of Swine," in Hafez, ed. *The Behavior of Domestic Animals* (Baltimore: Williams and Williams, 1969), pp. 349–390.

21. Thomas Luckmann makes this assertion in *Invisible Religion* (New York: Macmillan, 1967), p. 69. Parts of James Nelson's argument in *Embodiment* support this view as well. Sociobiology has some implications in relation to this assertion which I and other theologians may initially have ignored as denying human freedom. Perhaps that was simply another instance of theology's prejudice against the physical.

22. John Dewey, *Experience and Nature*, 2nd ed. (LaSalle, IL: Open Court Publishing, 1929), pp. 58–59, 100–101, 284–285.

23. Does the drive for meaning always involve relationships? Though I cannot argue the case here, that seems inevitable. It is true in part because sociality enters all aspects of one's being, even consciousness.

24. See Dorothee Soelle with Shirley A. Cloyes, *To Work and To Love: A Theology of Creation* (Philadelphia: Fortress Press, 1984), pp. 1–6, *passim*. Paul Ricoeur speaks of a "second naivete"; that might explain the contemporary resurgence of religious phenomena. See also Charles Birch, *A Purpose for Everything* (Mystic, CT: Twenty-third Publications, 1991).

25. Quoted in Charles Davis, *Body As Spirit: The Nature of Religious Feeling* (New York: Seabury, 1976), p. 11.

26. The full quote is: "Yet man, this part of your creation, wishes to praise you. You arouse him to take joy in praising you, for you have made us for yourself, and our heart is restless until it rests in you." *The Confessions of St. Augustine*, John K. Ryan, trans. (New York: Doubleday, 1960), p. 43.

27. *Institutes of the Christian Religion.* Ford Lewis Battles, trans., John T. McNeill, ed. (Philadelphia: Westminster Press, 1955), I, v., 5.

28. John Paul II, "Peace with God the Creator, Peace with All of Creation," World Day of Peace, January 1, 1990, no. 5.

29. Jay B. McDaniel, *Earth, Sky, Gods & Mortals: Developing An Ecological Spirituality* (Mystic, CT: Twenty-Third Publications, 1990), pp. 50–57. McDaniel has adopted this insight from his work with the Christian-Buddhist dialogue. Christian theologians whose work is compatible—in various ways—with this insight include Jonathan Edwards, Paul Tillich, and Karl Rahner.

30. Bill French's question, "Whose ozone layer?," if compared to "Which historical authority?" captures the different valorization criterion. See French, *op. cit.*, as compared to Alasdair McIntyre, *Whose Justice? Which Rationality?* (Notre Dame, Ind: University of Notre Dame Press, 1988). My point is that there are numerous tra-

ditions and histories, all important and insightful no doubt; nevertheless, there is only one ozone layer.

31. The broad parameters of this discussion preclude focusing on specific relations—as, for example, to animals. See, however, my article, "Animals in Christian Perspective," Strangers, Friends, or Kin? in Jay McDaniel and Charles Pinches, eds. *Good News for Animals?* (New York: Orbis Books, forthcoming).

32. McDaniel, *Earth, Sky, Gods & Mortals*, p. 166.

6. Homemaking

1. See Paul Wachtel, *The Psychology of Affluence*, and also John Paul II, *Centesimus Annus* (The One Hundreth Year), 1991, no. 37: "In his desire to have rather than be and to grow, man consumes the resources of the earth and his own life in an excessive and disordered way."

2. See, e.g., Pius XI, *Quadragesimo Anno* (The Reconstruction of the Social Order), 1931, and John Paul II, *Redemptor Hominis* (The Redeemer of Man), 1979, no. 16; *Centesimus Annus* (The One Hundredth Year), 1991, no. 38.

3. The media are especially to be held accountable here. Even though *Newsweek* is developing an environmental sensitivity, too often it still employs an adversarial framework in its reporting. See, for example, their article on "Return of the Wolf," August 12, 1991.

4. See my "Animals in Christian Perspective: Strangers, Friends, or Kin?" in McDaniel and Pinches, eds., *Good News for Animals?* One reason I limit my use of the language of rights is because it precludes a communitarian base; instead, it assumes a minimal or hostile relationship. On this point, see Elizabeth H. Wolgast, *The*

Grammar of Justice (Ithaca: Cornell University Press, 1987), especially Chapter Two.

5. Roger Shinn, ed. *Faith and Science in an Unjust World*, vol. 1 (Geneva: World Council of Churches, 1980) and Paul Abrecht, ed. *Faith and Science in an Unjust World*, vol. 2 (Geneva: World Council of Churches, 1980).

6. WCC, *Justice, Peace, Integrity of Creation*. Document No. 19, Geneva, Switzerland, March 1990, p. 11.

7. Gary Comstock, "The Value of Stewardship on the Face of the Earth," a lecture at Clarke College, April 1991, not yet published.

8. David Abram, "Merleau Ponty and the Voice of the Earth," *Environmental Ethics* 10:2 (Summer 1988), p. 107.

9. Ibid., pp. 112–115.

10. John Paul II, *Centesimus Annus*, May 2, *Origins* 21:1, May 16, 1991, p. 15.

11. Ibid.

12. McDaniel, *Earth, Sky, God, & Mortals*, p. 27.

13. Marnie Stetson, "People Who Live In Green Houses . . .", *World Watch* 4:5 (September- October 1991), p. 23.

14. Ibid.

15. See Jung, "Autonomy as Justice: Spatiality and the Revelation of Otherness," *Journal of Religious Ethics*, 1986.

16. See Robert Bellah, Richard Madsen, William M. Sullivan, Ann

Swidler, & Steven M. Tipton, *The Good Society* (New York: Knopf, 1991).

17. Concrete, practical suggestions for activities that promote a healthy environment can be found in Cummings, *Eco-Spirituality*, pp. 124–148; *365 Ways To Save The Planet*, a calendar from the Book of the Month Club; *Caring for Creation: Vision, Hope, and Justice*, a study booklet from the Evangelical Lutheran Church in America Environment Task Force, 1991; *Restoring Creation for Ecology and Justice*, The Presbyterian Church (USA), 1990; Loren Wilkinson, ed. *Earthkeeping in the Nineties: Stewardship of Creation*, Revised Edition. (Grand Rapids: Eerdmans Publishing Co., 1991), pp. 361–371; Jon Naar, *Design for a Livable Planet: How You Can Help Clean Up the Environment* (New York: Harper & Row, 1991); "Cut the Garbage," *USA Weekend* newspaper supplement, April 21–23, 1989; *Catholic Rural Life*, published by the National Catholic Rural Life Conference, Des Moines; the newsletter of the Land Stewardship Project, Marine, MN; *World Watch* magazine; etc.

In terms of Christian political action, see James A. Nash, *Loving Nature: Ecological Integrity and Christian Responsibility* (Nashville, TN: Abingdon Press, 1991), Chapter Eight. Lester Brown, ed. *State of the World 1992* (New York: W.W. Norton & Co., 1992) includes a number of articles on the politics of the environment.

7. Home Finances

1. This issue is beginning to be addressed. See especially Carol P. Robb and Carl J. Casebolt, eds. *Covenant For A New Creation: Ethics, Religion, and Public Policy* (Maryknoll, N.Y.: Orbis Books and GTU, 1991).

2. Aldo Leopold, *A Sand Country Almanac* (New York: Oxford University Press, 1949), p. vii.

3. Fred Kirschenmann writes that "Another reason farmers have

not been fully cognizant of ecology/economy connections is that not all the costs of current farming practices have been factored in. Expenditures for decontaminating ground water, restoring eroded soil, cleaning silt from ditches and drainages, or restoring lakes and streams contaminated by synthetic fertilizers and pesticides have been ignored in calculating the economics of conventional agriculture." See "The Ecology-Economy-Ethic Connection in Land Use," in Robb and Casebolt, eds., *Covenant For A New Creation*, p. 83.

4. Wendell Berry, *What Are People For?* (San Francisco: North Point Press, 1990), p. 206.

5. R. Bruce Douglas, *The Deeper Meaning of Economic Life* (Washington, D.C.: Georgetown University Press), p. xi.

6. See John Cobb and Herman Daly, *For the Common Good: Redirecting the Economy Toward Community, The Environment, and a Sustainable Future.* (Boston: Beacon Press, 1989), p. 111. The quote here is from an earlier draft.

7. *Science*, May 15, 1987, p. 769.

8. *Economic Justice For All* (Washington, D.C.: U.S. Catholic Conference, 1986).

9. Examples of how this anti-materialism affects theology are numerous. I believe Reinhold Niebuhr's emphasis on grace as pardon rather than as power can be attributed partly to this. The impact of this anti-materialism deserves further investigation.

10. Wendell Berry, *The Unsettling of America: Culture & Agriculture* (San Francisco: Sierra Club Books, 1978), Chapter Four.

11. W.H. Auden, *The Dyer's Hand* (London: Faber and Faber, 1963), p. 336.

12. Charles Cummings, *Eco-Spirituality: Toward A Reverent Life* (Mahwah, NJ: Paulist Press, 1991), pp. 3–26.

13. Wendell Berry, *The Unsettling of America*, p. 123.

14. Barbara Ehrenreich, "Why Don't We Like The Human Body?", *Time*, July 1, 1991, p. 80.

15. James Nelson, *Embodiment* (Minneapolis: Augsburg Publishing Company, 1978).

16. See Bruce Birch and Larry Rasmussen, *The Predicament of the Prosperous* (Philadelphia: Westminister Press, 1978).

17. See Rita Nakashima Brock, *Journey by Heart: A Christology of Erotic Power* (New York: Crossroad, 1988), and my article in *The Journal of Feminist Studies in Religion.*

18. See Charles K. Wilber and Roland Hoksbergen, "Ethical Values and Economic Theory: A Survey," *Religious Study Review* 12:3/4 (July/October 1986). Reinforcing this point is Robert Bellah, *et al.* "Taming the Market," *The Christian Century*, September 18–25, 1991, pp. 844–849.

19. Herman Daly, "Toward an Environmental Macroeconomics," *Land Economics* 67 (1991). The quote is from Mark Sagoff, "Nature Versus The Environment," *Report from the Institute for Philosophy and Public Policy* 11:3, Summer (1991), p. 7.

20. Philip Wogaman asserts, however, that *no* major economic system has adequately taken the environment into account. *The Great Economic Debate* (Philadelphia: Westminster Press, 1976). He does, however, mention a promising subsystem which he labels "Economic Conservationism."

21. Thomas Aquinas, *Summa Theologica*, trans. Fathers of the En-

glish Dominican Province (New York: Benzinger Brothers, 1947), Vol. One, Part One, Q. 47, Art. 2, p. 246. This insight is shared by the Orthodox, the Calvinist, and the Lutheran traditions.

22. Hugh of St. Victor, *Seven Books of Didactic Instruction*, Bk 7, Ch. 3; Migne, ed. *Patrologia Latina* 176:814.

23. The Catholic tradition which affirms the dignity of every person has, interestingly, often been articulated in Catholic thought on labor-management rights and responsibilities. See Oliver Williams and John Houck, *The Judeo-Christian Vision and the Modern Corporation* (Notre Dame, Ind.: University of Notre Dame Press, 1982).

24. The fact that levels of inequality and the actual numbers of people living in poverty are increasing is a matter of grave concern. See Kevin P. Phillips, *Politics of Rich & Poor: Wealth & the American Electorate in the Reagan Aftermath* (N.Y.: Random House, 1990).

25. Wendell Berry, *The Unsettling of America*, p. 138.

26. See Martin Seligman, "Depression and the Maximal Self," *Networker*, May/June 1991, pp. 32–33.

27. These images find some affinity with M. Douglas Meeks's view that "If we find no ready-made economic solutions to our dilemmas, we nevertheless find in the biblical traditions the shape of God's economy to which, for Christians, our economic systems should correspond as much as possible under the conditions of history." *God the Economist: The Doctrine of God and Political Economy* (Minneapolis: Fortress Press, 1989), p. 3.

28. Bellah, Madsen, Sullivan, Swidler, and Tipton, *The Good Society*, pp. 105, 106.

29. I am numbering all the benchmarks sequentially to indicate that they are cumulative steps toward the economy of God expressed in the theological moral vision.

30. What this might mean to persons could be measured: e.g., a decline in the number of homeless persons, lower crime rates, decline in rates of poverty, higher quality of air, lower rates of domestic abuse, lower divorce rates. Meeks, *op. cit.*, illustrates one implication in regard to economic growth: growth would be "a deepening of human capacities for the service of human development within community," p. 57.

What this means in terms of other species is not as obvious but is still measurable, I think: e.g., optimal population for habitat, freedom from disease, ability to enjoy natural inclinations, and physical *élan*.

31. At least they begin as motivational or dispositional guidelines. Every intention or evaluative perception can be structured in an institution (routinized) in such a way as to sustain the values it embodies. So, as Calvin taught us, even the Ten Commandments can be interpreted as a recommendation for the cultivation of certain virtues. Certainly Thomas' ethics was expressed largely as a system of virtues appropriate to eternal law.

32. See Meeks, *op. cit.*, Chapter Six. "God and Work." While I appreciate Meeks' work overall, I must say that his all-but-neglect of environmental issues calls for remediation.

33. See Meeks, Chapter Five. "God and Property." Also, Charles Avila, *Ownership: Early Christian Teaching* (Maryknoll: Orbis Books, 1983); *Summa Theologica*, II-II, q. 66, arts. 2 and 7. Gregory of Nyssa and the *Didache* express injunctions against absolute ownership as well.

34. It appears that God is, for the time being, sharing the power to shape creation. Human and natural processes seem to have predict-

able consequences, and we as a species have the power and foresight to shape the future. Although God is present, God seems to choose to work through natural processes and human reason and will-power. Human freedom is serious, i.e., has consequences. It is also obviously a responsible freedom.

35. Meeks, p. 77.

36. So Walter Brueggemann: "The central vision of world history in the Bible is that all creation is one, every creature in community with every other, living in harmony and security toward the joy and well-being of every other creature." *Living Toward A Vision: Biblical Reflections on Shalom* (Philadelphia: United Church Press, 1976), p. 15.

Epilogue

1. This history is condensed from Louise B. Young, "Easter Island: Scary Parable," *World Monitor* 4:8, August 1991, pp. 40–45.

2. For a list of some of these, see footnote 18 of chapter 6.

3. There are a few fine resources emerging: Elizabeth Roberts and Elias Amidon, eds. *Earth Prayers from Around the World* (San Francisco: Harper San Francisco, 1991); Mary Jo Valenziano, *Rogation Days* (Oak Park, IL: Catholic Conference of Illinois, 1989); Victoria M. Tufano, ed. *Rural Life Prayers, Blessings and Liturgies* (Des Moines: National Catholic Rural Life Conference, 1989); *Environmental Sabbath, Earth Rest Day*, United Nations Environment Programme, 1990. We at the Center for Theology and Land intend to publish a book of rural liturgies in the near future.

4. Russell E. Train, "Religion and the Environment," *Journal of Forestry* (September 1991), p. 15.

5. The University of Wisconsin Student Union at Madison offers reusable mugs and charges 20% less to fill them. This saves 8,000 styrofoam cups **weekly**.

6. A majority of local U.S. congregations are directly involved in addressing health-care needs in their communities. "Congregations and Health," *The Christian Century*, December 11, 1991, p. 1159.

7. John Hart, *The Spirit of the Earth: A Theology of the Land* (New York: Paulist Press, 1984) has a particularly good list of political suggestions. See pp. 141–148.

Index

Abram, David, 153
Acts, 34, 62, 65, 78, 128, 147
Agriculture, 33, 94, 141, 154, 155
Air, 9, 10, 12, 14, 27, 31, 43, 51, 63, 108, 149, 157; Conditioning, 12, 14, 24; Pollution, 10, 26
Alienation, 42
Animals, 1, 2, 5, 6, 11, 47, 49, 64, 65, 68, 79, 81, 82, 85, 86, 88, 94, 95, 96, 98, 99, 108, 133, 134, 146, 150, 151, 152
Anthropocentrism, 43, 61
Anti-materialism, 111, 155
Aquinas, St. Thomas, 116, 156
Atmosphere, 2, 5, 7, 8, 11, 12, 13, 99
Augustine, St., 83, 126, 151
Austin, Richard Cartwright, 143, 144, 146
Autonomy, 23, 84, 125, 150, 153

Barney, Gerald, 15, 16, 138
Beauty, 4, 20, 47, 48, 49, 52, 54, 71, 82, 131, 140, 144
Bellah, Robert, 23, 140, 153, 156, 157
Berry, Wendell, 68, 75, 108, 111, 118, 149, 156, 157
Bible, 55, 59, 60, 61, 62, 71, 143, 146, 158
Biosphere, 7, 9, 11, 15, 17, 21, 33, 45, 52, 70, 85, 95, 99, 122
Birch, Bruce, 138, 151, 156
Blessing, 62, 63, 68, 148
Blood, 9, 10, 41, 79
Body, 5, 9, 29, 31, 32, 42, 70, 72, 76, 77, 78, 79, 80, 83, 96, 98, 99, 103, 111, 112, 113, 114, 115, 132, 150, 155; Functions, 77, 78; Systems, 7, 9, 10, 14, 16, 97
Brain, 9, 77, 78, 79, 83, 150
Breathing, 5, 7, 8, 9, 11, 19, 26, 79
Brock, Rita Nakashima, 156